KABBALAH
FOR
BEGINNERS

KABBALAH
FOR
BEGINNERS

UNDERSTANDING AND APPLYING
KABBALISTIC HISTORY, CONCEPTS,
AND PRACTICES

BRIAN YOSEF SCHACHTER-BROOKS

ROCKRIDGE
PRESS

Interior and Cover Designer: Patricia Fabricant
Art Producer: Sara Feinstein
Editor: Lia Ottaviano
Production Editor: Rachel Taenzler

All Illustrations used under license from Creative Market/kloroform.
Author photo courtesy of © Florian Kuster.

ISBN: Print 978-1-64739-003-7 | eBook 978-1-64739-004-4

R0

For Lisa, with
tremendous gratitude
for supporting this
writing with strength
and grace.

CONTENTS

INTRODUCTION

I was raised in a very secular home, but from a young age I was drawn to anything spiritual–astrology, tarot cards, astral projection, mysticism, magic, anything I could get my hands on. Between seventh and eighth grade, I was invited by my friend's family to travel to Europe. When we were in England, I expanded my occult book collection, and began to notice references to something called the "Tree of Life," which was part of something called "Kabbalah."

I didn't know what Kabbalah was, but there was something strangely familiar about it. As I continued to read, I eventually realized Kabbalah was Jewish. Though I knew very little about my own heritage, I always had a sense there was something very deep about Judaism, as if there were a "hidden light" beneath the surface, just barely visible.

As I studied Western occultism, I was blown away to see that this Jewish spirituality, Kabbalah, played a huge part.

I felt compelled to learn more about this wisdom from my own heritage, but I didn't know where to look. So, I kept learning about Kabbalah from non-Jewish sources, until one day I went to visit my Uncle Howard. He and his family, my Aunt Marion and my cousins, were observant Jews. I spent the night at their house in Highland Park, New Jersey, and I brought along a pile of my mystical books.

That night, as I slept, Uncle Howard pored over all my books. In the morning, he proceeded to show me how much of what I had been studying was present in Torah and Judaism.

He then took me to a local Jewish bookstore and bought me my first introductory book on Kabbalah.

I remember bringing that book with me everywhere, devouring it as much as I could regardless of what was going on around me.

That was the beginning of my connection with the world of Kabbalah; it started with a general interest in spirituality, where I discovered the impression Kabbalah made on me and the world in general, and led me back to discover the esoteric dimension of my own tradition.

But even after I discovered Kabbalah, I continued to study many different traditions and practices throughout my childhood; I had a yearning to find some kind of ultimate Truth or answer. It was a search for God, for enlightenment, for awakening.

When I was 18, I had an awakening experience that finally satisfied what I was looking for:

It was the summer of 1987. I had just graduated from high school, and I was talking with a friend about an ethical problem: Another friend of ours had stolen a test tube from my father's medical clinic to hold little things in her purse. Although the test tube was probably worth a few cents, I was bothered by the fact that she stole it, and I couldn't figure out why I was bothered. If you steal something and no one is hurt or even notices, is there anything wrong with that?

Clearly, this kind of stealing wouldn't hurt anyone. But what would it do to the one who is stealing? Where does the motivation to steal come from? In the act of stealing, what are you actually *living for*?

As we came to this point in our conversation, something incredible happened to both of us simultaneously. It was as if our hearts had accidentally caught fire.

"You've got to live for God!" we cried.

Something inside me broke open; all negativity, worry, and fear simply dropped away, and suddenly there was this light pouring through me. I was completely free, and I was "on fire" to "live for God" alone.

But it didn't last; within a few weeks I was back to being the old me, except that I'd had this incredible experience, and I wanted more!

That was the beginning of taking on traditional Jewish practices and learning in a more focused way. It was also the beginning of my relationship with Reb Zalman Schachter-Shalomi, *z"l*, who became my long-term mentor and *rebbe* from 1987 until he died in 2014.

For years, I studied and practiced, but I didn't find my way back to the simplicity of that awakening I had experienced until 1998, at which point my efforts had finally "come to fruit," as Reb Zalman reflected to me. The key, I discovered, was the application of awareness to present moment experience (nowadays this is called mindfulness, Presence, or wakefulness). It is from this understanding that I began to write and teach on Judaism, meditation, and consciousness in the San Francisco Bay Area in 2006. In 2016, I founded *Torah of Awakening* as an online community for spiritual transformation through Kabbalah-based teachings and practices.

Kabbalah is a vast and complex ocean of knowledge and tradition. In this book, I have attempted to accomplish two things.

First and foremost, I want to give you, the reader, a taste of the essence of Kabbalah as a path to inner freedom. This is the thread that runs through the whole book, and my hope is that you will not merely absorb the information in these pages, but will be motivated to continue uncovering the eternal dimension of your own deepest being.

Second, I want to give you a foundation of knowledge about the history, personalities, texts, and teachings of Kabbalah that will serve as a base from which you may continue your studies.

As you move through this book, these two levels–the informational level and the experiential level–are woven together so that you don't spend too much time with the information without taking a dip into the experiential. I bless you, that you should find what you seek in these pages: both food for the mind and for the soul. Let's begin!

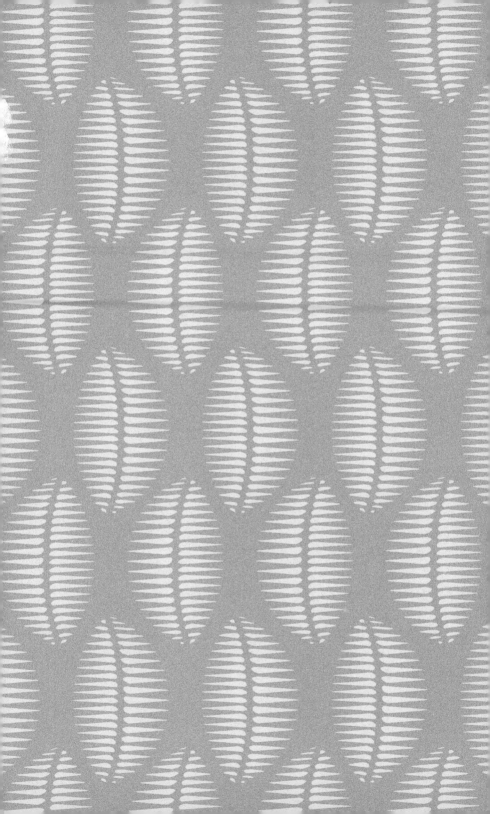

WHAT IS KABBALAH?

n this chapter you will get a taste of Kabbalah from three different angles. First and most importantly, we'll look at the purpose and goal of Kabbalah, and how it relates to Judaism. We'll also examine some of the misconceptions that exist about Kabbalah in today's popular spiritual culture. Second, we'll look at the key figures, both historical and legendary, who make up the pantheon of Kabbalistic personalities in the tradition. Third, we'll look at the key texts through which Kabbalah has evolved throughout history and seek to understand how they relate to one another.

Before we jump in, it will be helpful to understand an essential feature of Kabbalah (as well as many other mystical traditions) that fundamentally differs from ordinary, non-mystical religion: the understanding of what is meant by "God."

In mainstream traditional Judaism, God is, for lack of a better term, a kind of supernatural being, the Creator of the Universe and Lawgiver of the Jewish people.

This is not quite so in Kabbalah.

While conceptions of God differ somewhat in the many expressions of Kabbalah throughout history, there are certain Kabbalistic constants. First and foremost, God is the *Ayn Sof,* "without end" or "Infinite" in Hebrew. As the Infinite, there can be nothing outside of It; therefore, It includes everything, and everything is part of God.

This understanding is implied in the most central Name of God in Hebrew. This traditionally unpronounceable Name is composed of four Hebrew letters, *Yod, Hei, Vav,* and *Hei,* which could be transliterated into the English letters Y-H-V-H. These letters come from the Hebrew root of the verb "to be." The message, as the Kabbalists understood, is that God is not *a* being, not even the most supreme being, but is rather Being Itself. God does not exist; *God is Existence.* God is the is-ness, present in all things, but is Itself not a thing; therefore, God is also called *ayin,* which means no-thing, or literally "there is not" in Hebrew.

Once we understand this, it follows that God is not in any way remote, but is immediately available to us, as it says in the Torah:

For this thing is very close to you, in your mouth and in your heart, to do it!

DEUTERONOMY 30:14

In other words, the Divine is an intrinsic dimension of our experience right now, and we can become aware of and connect with this dimension *if* we know how to do it. This book will help you do just that.

This can be challenging, however. Because most of us are so conditioned to think of God as a separate entity, it can be difficult to grasp this mystical conception of the Divine and apply it practically. For this reason, I'll seek to reinforce this understanding again and again, for it is totally impossible to understand Kabbalah or the transformational process available to us without really getting this basic point.

WHAT IS KABBALAH?

The human was driven out of the Garden, and the cherubim and the fiery, ever-turning sword were stationed east of Eden to guard the way to the Tree of Life . . .

GENESIS 3:24

Who are we?

The Torah paints a picture of humanity originating in the "Garden"–a state of balance and harmony. Somehow, we stepped out of that primal harmony; we became separated from the "Tree of Life." And although humanity has gone through many monumental transformations throughout our history, our basic condition remains: a felt sense that we are somehow separate, out of place, out of alignment with reality. That lack of alignment expresses itself in the many horrors we humans are guilty of committing against ourselves, each other, and the world.

The great spiritual traditions are remedies for our basic condition; they are guides pointing the way back to primal harmony, that simple and innocent aliveness we so long for. The story of the Garden of Eden resonates so deeply because we all experienced that simple and joyful aliveness in our infancy. It is deep in our collective memory; we know on some level that it is real, but the "flaming sword" of our minds and emotions seems to block the way.

Kabbalah is one of the great spiritual traditions. It emerges from the same lineage that brought us the ancient story of the expulsion from Eden, and it comes to show us the way back to the Garden, back to the Tree of Life.

The word "Kabbalah" comes from the Hebrew root which means "to receive," because it was originally taught only from master to disciple. Since Kabbalah is rooted in the "inner" or "esoteric" dimension of Judaism (as opposed to the more common outer, or "exoteric" dimension), Kabbalists felt their teachings were best communicated directly to a student that was ready to be a *mekubal*–that is, to receive its wisdom.

But what is this "inner" or "esoteric" dimension?

When a musician reads and plays music from the page, we could say that they are involved mostly with the outer dimension of music. A composer, on the other hand, creates music from within themselves, seemingly out of nothing, and is therefore involved with the inner dimension of music.

It's the same with many areas of human activity. A person who cooks by following a recipe is involved with the outer dimension of cooking; a chef who innovates a dish with whatever ingredients are available is operating from the inner dimension.

Similarly, while external Judaism is primarily concerned with what God said in the sacred texts, the Kabbalist is primarily concerned with connecting to God directly. While external Judaism proclaims the creed that "God is One," the Kabbalist seeks to know this Oneness experientially. While external Judaism tells the story of the Exodus from slavery in Egypt, the Kabbalist seeks inner freedom from negativity, from psychological limitation, and ultimately from separateness—from the sense of being separated from our deepest Divine nature, from the "Tree of Life" within.

In fact, just as the story of the Exodus is central to Judaism, inner freedom is really the central theme of Kabbalah. The Exodus is the primary allegory for inner freedom, but there are other freedom narratives as well. For example, in Lurianic Kabbalah (which we will look at in chapter 2), there's the idea that Divine energy is "trapped" in physical matter, and that our task is to liberate these "Divine sparks" through our spiritual work. Earlier, I mentioned that the experience of inner freedom I had when I was 18 didn't fully ripen until 1998. Here's something that happened during that time that I consider to be my first liberation of those trapped "sparks":

I was driving my car and approaching an intersection when another car suddenly cut me off. Instantly, I was filled with rage, but I suddenly realized this was a crucial opportunity to practice being present with the emotion. I brought awareness into deep connection with the anger. It was very painful at first, but then the anger seemed to move like smoke up through the body and out the top of my head. It was as if the energy trapped within the emotion of anger was set free.

After a few seconds, everything looked completely different to me. I could see that the driver who cut me off was actually helping me. It dawned on me that everything I was perceiving— the caw of a crow soaring through the sky, the road glistening with moisture from a recent rain, the bustling traffic—all of it was part of one reality. All of it was arising within and not separate from my awareness. Then I realized: *I am this awareness. I am not separate from any of this.*

That moment was a turning point for me. It showed me that movement toward inner freedom is something that can be practiced constantly, by becoming present with whatever is happening in the moment.

Of course, dividing things into "inner" and "outer" isn't so cut and dry. A musician who reads notes from a page is also interpreting the notes, connecting with the intention of the composer, and expressing a certain feeling in the playing. In this way, they too are connected with the inner dimension. Composers also have to deal with the mechanics of notation, music theory, and so on, and are therefore involved with the outer dimension to some degree. These "inner" and "outer" dimensions of Judaism are similarly intertwined.

In order for the practice of Judaism (or any religion or tradition) to be alive and meaningful, practitioners need to be connected to both its inner and outer reality. Still, there is a difference between the Jew who is concerned primarily with rules of conduct, beliefs, customs, and stories (outer), and the Jew who is concerned primarily with living in connection with their Divine Essence (inner). There were even times in history when the ordinary, externally-focused rabbis felt threatened by this difference. After all, they thought, if someone has their own connection with the Divine, perhaps they might attract their own followers and go against the accepted norms of the tradition. (And sometimes they did!)

For this reason, throughout history, Kabbalah has sometimes been at odds with normative, exoteric Judaism. There are several instances of Kabbalists being shunned as heretics and even excommunicated, as in the way the mainstream rabbis of the 18th century railed against the Baal Shem Tov and Hasidism (more on this in chapter 6). Still, Kabbalah is and always has been an integral part of Judaism, not an offshoot, as Christianity became. With the exception of a few heretical movements and flowerings of Kabbalah in non-Jewish circles, Kabbalists have been committed practitioners of normative Judaism; their mysticism has almost always served to add depth and meaning to the exoteric practices, not eliminate them. Inner and outer are, after all, complementary—two sides of one coin—though their historical relationship with each other hasn't always been easy.

At the same time, the underlying *principles* of Kabbalah aren't dependent on practicing Judaism. Ultimately, Kabbalah points us to a direct connection with the truth of who we are, and anyone can apply its principles to discover this deepest dimension of our own being, regardless of religious belief or practice.

WHAT KABBALAH IS NOT

Before we explore what Kabbalah is in greater detail, it will be helpful to understand a little bit about what Kabbalah is not. Kabbalah has become popular in contemporary spiritual culture, and because of this, some misconceptions have become common. These misconceptions are not always entirely wrong, but they tend to miss certain nuances.

For example, one common misconception is that Kabbalah is an "ancient spiritual system."

Again, this is not completely wrong. Kabbalah is rooted in Judaism, which is certainly of very ancient origin. But the body of wisdom we call Kabbalah didn't emerge in writing until the 12th century.

As we saw earlier, Kabbalah was first communicated orally, not through texts, so we don't know exactly when it started. The earliest Kabbalistic texts refer to an oral tradition upon which the teachings and symbols of Kabbalah are based, so we know it existed for some time, though we don't know exactly when or how this oral tradition developed.

Furthermore, Kabbalah isn't a single system. Rather, there are many different systems that are part of Kabbalah (such as Theosophical Kabbalah, Ecstatic Kabbalah, and Hasidic Kabbalah, all of which we will explore in chapter 5). These systems are related in that they share a common language, symbols, and texts, but their interpretations of these shared commonalities differ. As we move through this book, we will explore a number of different expressions of Kabbalah (and pre-Kabbalah) throughout history and get a taste of what sets them apart from one another, as well as what unites them.

Another misconception, born from the way Kabbalah is sometimes marketed nowadays, is that Kabbalah is a pathway to self-improvement—to find your soulmate, to increase your income, or to achieve better health—rather than a pathway to spiritual transformation.

Again, this isn't completely untrue. Kabbalah is about discovering and living in connection with the deepest level of your being: the level that the tradition calls Divine. Kabbalah is, therefore, a transformative path, changing the way we experience our own existence. When we transform on this deep level, that transformation often does help us in other ways as well. It may inspire more charisma, and therefore help us in the soulmate department. It may also dissolve certain mental and emotional blocks that were keeping us from reaching our physical or financial potential. But these things were never the point. Kabbalah has always been a path of spiritual transformation, not a pathway to materialistic gain.

Finally, on the opposite end of the spectrum, there is a common misconception that Kabbalah should only be studied by married males who are over the age of 40. This is more a reflection of the traditional culture within which Kabbalah arose; study of the Torah was, until the 20th century, almost exclusively a male activity.

However, being 40 was never an essential condition for learning Kabbalah. Interestingly, one of the greatest Kabbalists of all time, Isaac Luria, died before he was 40, and his teacher, Moshe Cordovero, wrote his seminal book, *Pardes Rimonim*, when he was only 28!

It's important to know that Kabbalah has its origins in the very traditional world of Medieval and pre-Medieval Rabbinic Judaism, a world of strict gender roles and religiously pre-scribed lifestyles. But Kabbalah is much deeper than the beliefs and mores of any particular time period. Anyone drawn to the unique spirituality of Kabbalah will be able to partake of its life-giving waters, regardless of gender or background.

EVERYDAY KABBALAH

MEDITATION:

Bring to mind that your nervous system is like a vast Tree of Life within, with roots and branches spreading throughout your body. It vibrates with aliveness and the bliss of simply being, but the "flaming sword" of your thoughts and feelings can cover over this simple radiance.

As long as you struggle against your thoughts and feelings, they only become more powerful. Instead, allow your thoughts to be there; allow your feelings to be there. Feel them completely, and welcome whatever comes into your mind. Don't get drawn into your thoughts; let them come, then let them go. Instead of thinking, focus your attention on whatever is present, right now.

Feel your breathing. Listen. Feel whatever is here to be felt. Spend a few minutes connecting with your inner Tree of Life, being aware of whatever is arising in the present moment. Then, when you're ready, return to your day's activities, refreshed and renewed to engage with life in a more present state.

KEY FIGURES IN KABBALAH

The flavor of any spiritual tradition is colored by the characters–both historical and legendary–who comprise the story of how the tradition was created, transmitted, and transformed. A study of Kabbalah wouldn't be complete without meeting the characters through which this tradition comes to us.

ADAM

And Hashem Elohim placed Adam in the Garden of Eden, to till it and tend it . . .

GENESIS 2:15

The Torah recalls how God created the first human, called Adam, from the dust of the earth. The Hebrew word *adam* means "human being," and *adamah* means "red earth" or "clay."

The first human being's name, then, was something like "Earth Human." Adam is the primordial human: a symbol, in a sense, of all people and of the human condition. In fact, according to tradition, the souls of all humans who would ever live were contained within the soul of Adam.

The Biblical story relates how Adam was first alone, and then Eve was created from his rib. But, according to a Kabbalistic understanding of this story, Adam was originally androgynous, both male and female. The creation of Eve, according to this version, was the separation of the *Adam* into its male and female components.

The inner message is, again, the theme of separation. Once upon a time, to be human was to be Whole. That Wholeness was fractured; male and female became separate, and both became separate from their essence, and therefore from the Tree of Life.

But there is a way back to Wholeness. As human beings find their way back home, one by one, soul by soul, the primordial human (Adam) too comes back into Wholeness, until all of humanity is transformed. This Jewish vision of the future in which humanity will eventually become fully transformed is called the "Messianic Era." The whole human project, from a Kabbalistic perspective, forms a long arc through history with Adam on one end and *Moshiakh* (Messiah) on the other.

ABRAHAM

Go for yourself from your land, from your relatives . . . to the land I will show you . . .

GENESIS 12:1

To understand Abraham and the central role he plays, let's go back to the first sentence of the Torah:

In the beginning of Elohim's creating of the heavens and the earth . . . The Divine Name *Elohim* literally means "gods," a plural word! But it is conjugated as a singular noun. This would be like saying in English, "Gods is creating."

Judaism arose out of the deeply polytheistic culture of the ancient Near East. The hint in this opening Biblical line is that the ancient Hebrews were not saying their god is the most powerful of all the gods. Nor were they saying that their god is the only god. Rather, they were saying that all the gods are actually a Unity; the manifold forces of the universe comprise a singular Being whose Name is "Gods."

This was the original impulse of Judaism. The rich multiplicity of reality is not merely a drama of conflicting and harmonizing elements; it is also a Unity, a Single reality, and it is toward that Unity that we should direct our aspirations and motivations. It is to that Oneness that we should sing our praises.

According to legend, Abraham was the first to recognize this Oneness in the midst of a pagan world. The Divine message that came to him—to leave his family and set out for a new land—was a message to begin a new spiritual culture that would eventually give rise to the great monotheistic traditions of the West.

In Kabbalah, however, Abraham is more than a historical or legendary figure; he is, along with several other Biblical characters, the embodiment of a particular spiritual quality. Later in this book we will explore the various spiritual qualities in more depth. For now, let's briefly recount the lineage of Abraham that gave rise to these archetypal personalities:

Abraham and Sarah miraculously had their son Isaac in their old age. Isaac and his wife Rebecca had Jacob, who received the second name "Israel" from an angel. Jacob/Israel had twelve sons who were the founders of the "Twelve Tribes of Israel."

The eleventh son, Joseph, was most beloved by Israel. Out of jealousy, his brothers tried to kill Joseph and ended up selling him into slavery. Joseph went through many harsh trials, but with his Divinely inspired talent for interpreting dreams, he eventually rose to the rank of Pharaoh's highest-level advisor. When a famine ravaged the land, Joseph was able to bring his father Jacob/Israel, his brothers, and his extended family into Egypt, where he sustained them with food through the famine.

Once in Egypt, the twelve tribes thrived and prospered. Eventually, a new Pharaoh arose who was fearful of the Children of Israel, so he enslaved them all in an effort to oppress them and diminish their power and fertility.

And that brings us to the next key figure in our survey of Kabbalistic figures: Moses.

MOSES

And the Divine said, "I have seen the plight of
My people in Egypt and have heard their outcry
because of their taskmasters; for I have known their
sufferings . . . "

EXODUS 3:7

If Abraham was the first patriarch of the Jewish people and the
founder of its spiritual core, Moses was first to be a political
and spiritual leader, establishing the Hebrew tribes as a unified
nation under the Divine Unity that Abraham proclaimed.
Abraham was called to establish a bloodline and a teaching,
but Moses was called to lead the descendants of that bloodline
from slavery to freedom. Abraham was the progenitor of many
peoples; Moses gathered in the dispossessed of many peoples,
together with the Children of Israel, and forged a new people:

The Israelites journeyed . . . and also, a mixed
multitude went up with them . . .

EXODUS 12:37-38

While exoteric Judaism tends to be oriented toward the
historical aspect of its scriptures, Kabbalah is oriented toward
their inner reality. On this level, the Exodus from Egypt is a
metaphor pointing to the movement from inner bondage (the
constrictions of anger, fear, and neediness) to spiritual liberation (spaciousness, joy, and peace).

We can see this encoded in the words themselves: The word
for Egypt, Mitzrayim, comes from the Hebrew root that means
"narrow" or "constricted," probably because Egypt was a

narrow country, built up along the Nile. But on a spiritual level, this points to the experience of inner constriction, of being trapped by painful and reactive emotions. On the deepest level, it is being trapped in a narrow identity created by our thoughts and feelings: the ego.

The movement from Egypt to freedom, then, is the movement from ego to inner spaciousness; from negativity to gratitude; from the stressful demands of time to the restfulness of the present moment.

And the present moment is always with us! Spiritual liberation is ever-available if we know how to become present. (The exercises in this book are designed to help you make that shift.) This is also why Moses, the liberator, was also the first lawgiver, transmitting a stream of "commandments," called *mitzvot*, from the Divine to the people. From a Kabbalistic perspective, all of the *mitzvot* can be seen as "exercises" for affecting inner liberation. Thus, if Egypt symbolizes slavery to our lowest impulses, the Law of Moses represents the freedom to serve our highest aspirations.

This movement from bondage to freedom is embodied in the earliest commandments given to the people: The first 20 commandments in the Torah are all *mitzvot* that relate to the celebration of freedom, the "Passover." The very next one is the *mitzvah* of the Sabbath: that one day per week, the demands of time are suspended, and for 25 hours life is to be lived in spacious celebration and honoring of the world as it is, with no "work" being done.

According to tradition, Moses was the first of hundreds, perhaps thousands of Hebrew prophets. But then, somewhere around 500 BCE, the age of the prophets came to an end, and Jewish spiritual leadership began to transition from those who channeled Divine messages to those who studied the texts in which those messages were recorded. The Bible was fixed and canonized, and a new kind of spiritual literature started to blossom: the writings of the scholars and interpreters of scripture. The age of the Rabbis had begun.

AKIVA

Although much rabbinic writing is concerned with Jewish law, called *halakhah* (literally, "the way" or "the walk"), the rabbis were also a link in the chain of spirituality that emerged from the earliest prophets and eventually found full expression in the Kabbalah in the Middle Ages. There are two particularly significant rabbinic personalities who served to embody and transmit the esoteric stream of the tradition. The first of these is Rabbi Akiva.

Rabbi Akiva lived from around the year 50 to 135 CE. He was a leading sage and a major personality in the Mishna, the earliest rabbinic text. According to tradition, he edited and established the final form of the Sefer Yetzirah, a pre-Kabbalah mystical text traditionally ascribed to Abraham that we will look at later in this book.

Legend has it that he was descended from converts, and that although he was a poor and uneducated shepherd, he married a wealthy woman who supported him through his rabbinic learning, which didn't start until he was 40 years old. He was inspired to begin his journey of learning when he noticed that a certain stone in a well had become hollow from the persistent drippings from buckets. He thought to himself, "If little drips of water can penetrate this solid stone over time, how much more so can words of Torah penetrate this human heart?"

The Talmud—the most important rabbinic text dating from the sixth century CE—tells of a mystical incident in which Rabbi Akiva entered the "orchard" (the Garden of Eden) with three other rabbis. One of them became a heretic, one went insane, and one perished; only Rabbi Akiva "came in peace and left in peace."

Rabbi Akiva was also a martyr, brutally murdered at the hands of the Romans. The story goes that as he was tortured to death, he calmly chanted the core of Jewish liturgy, the *Sh'ma:* "Hear Israel, the Divine is our God, the Divine is One." He perished as he chanted the final word *ekhad,* "One," and his martyrdom gave rise to a core Kabbalistic teaching that one should surrender one's ego and one's sense of separate self when chanting the *Sh'ma.*

We will look at the *Sh'ma* in depth in chapter 4.

RABBI SHIMON

Rabbi Shimon bar Yokhai, one of the only two students of Rabbi Akiva to be ordained as rabbis, is perhaps the most well-known early rabbinic figure in Kabbalah. A great sage of the second century who lived during Roman rule, legend says that he authored the Zohar: the "bible" of Kabbalah that appeared in 13th-century Spain.

A story in the Talmud tells that a governor during the reign of emperor Antoninus Pius decreed that Rabbi Shimon be put to death after rumors spread that he had bad-mouthed the Romans. Rabbi Shimon and his son, Rabbi Eliezer, hid in a cave where a carob tree and a well of water miraculously appeared. They would take off their clothes, bury themselves in sand up to their necks, and study Torah all day long. When the time for prayer would come, they would get dressed, say their prayers, then remove their clothes again and bury themselves as before. In this way their clothes never wore out, and they stayed alive by eating from the carob tree and drinking from the well.

After 12 years, the spirit of Elijah the prophet came and told them that the emperor had died and it was safe to come out of hiding. They emerged from the cave and saw someone plowing a field. Rabbi Shimon became angry that someone would neglect the study of Torah by engaging in mundane work; fire shot from his eyes and incinerated the farmer. A voice from heaven then admonished him to get back to his cave. He had to stay there for another 12 months to integrate the heights he had reached during the 12 years before he could again function safely in the world.

This legend highlights the dual nature of mystical transformation. At first, there is a disidentification from our normal concept of the world; what we thought was reality is shown to be a sham, and our illusory concepts "incinerate" in the fire of awareness. But that experience is not the end; there must then be an integration process by which one learns to come back to ordinary reality, to bring the blessing of that awareness back into the world.

MOSES DE LEÓN, MOSES CORDOVERO, AND ISAAC LURIA

The prophetic period and the early rabbinic period contained an esoteric dimension of teaching and practice that became the foundation of Kabbalah, but the writings we identify as Kabbalah didn't emerge until the Middle Ages. Its most central work, known as the Zohar, didn't emerge until the 13th century.

The Zohar was the crown jewel of medieval Jewish mysticism. It was first circulated by the Castilian Kabbalist Moses de León, who claimed he had come to possess a manuscript that was authored by the great second-century Rabbi Shimon bar Yohai.

The ambiguous and poetic nature of the Zohar, in combination with its inspirational beauty and popularity, begged for interpretation and explanation. In the coming centuries, many Kabbalists would publish their own takes on the Zohar, giving rise to several different systems of Kabbalah that shared a common root. Of all the different Zohar-based systems, perhaps the most prominent was the one contained in the works of Rabbi Moses ben Jacob Cordovero. Cordovero was a 16th-century Kabbalist who lived in the small city of Sefad, a mystical center of Kabbalah set on a hill in the upper Galilee.

Around the same time, a young rabbi in Jerusalem named Isaac Luria discovered the Zohar. At the age of 22, he was so captivated by the mysticism of the Zohar that he became a hermit, living alone in a small cottage on the bank of the Nile while he immersed himself in the Zohar for 13 years. In 1569 he moved to Sefad, where he studied briefly with Moses Cordovero. After Cordovero's death, Luria was acknowledged as the new master, attracting a devoted circle of disciples.

Luria came to be known as the Ari, which means the "Lion." He wrote very little—just a few poems in Aramaic—but his disciples shared his teachings extensively, recording them from his spontaneous lectures. Those teachings became known as the "Lurianic Kabbalah," and most Kabbalah today derives in some way from the lineage of those teachings.

SHABBETAI TZVI

Shabbetai Tzvi was born in 1626 into a wealthy Turkish family. He was given a traditional rabbinic education, but, like Luria, he became obsessed with Kabbalah in his late teens and began attracting followers.

As I mentioned at the beginning of this chapter, the overarching theme of Kabbalah is transformation, variously called redemption, salvation, or liberation. While this speaks to a universal human predicament, Judaism came to see this in the particularistic experience of the Jewish people: an experience characterized by exile, powerlessness, and oppression, ultimately culminating in the future coming of a Messiah, *Moshiakh,* who would lead the Jewish people back to their land and herald a new age of peace and universal recognition of the Divine.

Given this belief in messianism, it is understandable that in the course of Jewish history, charismatic spiritual leaders with messianic claims would sometimes appear. The case of Jesus and Christianity was one such example. In the 17th century, there arose perhaps the most historically significant messianic claim since Jesus.

About 100 years after the Ari, European Jewry was in crisis. Nearly 100,000 Jews were murdered in the grizzly pogroms of Bohdan Khmelnytsky—about a third of the Jewish population. There was a ripeness for the promise of salvation, and it was into this atmosphere that Shabbetai Tzvi began proclaiming himself to be the long-awaited messiah.

He declared himself the messiah in 1648, after which he was banished from his hometown and began traveling through Greece and Turkey. Eventually he settled in Egypt, and for some time he lived a quiet, reclusive life, seemingly abandoning his messianic claims. But everything changed when he met Rabbi Nathan of Gaza, a Kabbalist who claimed to have had a vision that Shabbetai Tzvi was, in fact, the messiah. Nathan eventually convinced Shabbetai Tzvi of his messiah-hood, and thus began a mass movement that swept Europe, with Shabbetai Tzvi at the center.

In 1666, Shabbetai Tzvi was arrested in Constantinople, after which he was offered the choice of either trial by arrows, being impaled, or converting to Islam. He chose to convert, and became Aziz Mehmed Effendi.

While some communities of his followers continued to exist, for most of European Jewry, Shabbetai Tzvi had wounded the reputation of Kabbalah and caused many Jews to lose faith altogether; a healing was needed. It was into this post-Shabbatian world that a new kind of Kabbalah came onto the scene to fill this crucial need. This new Kabbalah became known as Hasidism.

Hasidism is perhaps the most influential movement of Jewish spirituality to this day; its genius was to express the essence of Kabbalah with simplicity and directness, to make it available for the common person. In chapter 5 we will dive into Hasidism in depth.

KABBALISTIC TEXTS

In Judaism, the prohibition against iconography and other religious art, as well as the prolonged historical reality of exile, caused the textual tradition to take a more primary role than in perhaps any other tradition. In this section we'll take a deeper look at the foundational texts of Kabbalah throughout history and how the tradition evolved through them.

TORAH

> Give ear, O heavens, and I will speak!
> Let the earth hear the words of my mouth!
> May my teaching drip like rain,
> My words flow like dew,
> Like showers on young growth, like droplets
> on grass . . .
>
> DEUTERONOMY 32:1-2

The word "Torah," which literally translates to "teaching," has multiple meanings. On the simple level, Torah is the first five books of the Jewish (as well as Christian) Bible: Genesis, Exodus, Leviticus, Numbers, and Deuteronomy. Genesis begins with the creation story, then briefly narrates the origins of different peoples and languages, including the story of the "great flood" and Noah's ark. It then focuses on the origins of the Hebrews, culminating in the descent of the Children of Israel into Egypt, where they were enslaved.

The rest of the Torah, Exodus through Deuteronomy, focuses on Moses leading the Children of Israel out of Egypt to freedom, receiving the Torah on Mt. Sinai, and their journey through the wilderness to the Promised Land. (The traditional view is that all five books of the Torah were received by Moses on Sinai, even though many of the events narrated in the Torah hadn't happened yet!)

In a broader sense, Torah includes the entire Bible, as well as all the rabbinic commentaries composed of wisdom (*aggadah*), legends (*midrashim*), practical laws (*halakhah*), and eventually, mysticism (*Kabbalah*).

On the most comprehensive level, Torah includes any authentic spiritual teaching that anyone might teach, even spontaneously, or even spiritual wisdom that one might gain from an experience or situation. In other words, at least potentially, *everything is Torah*. And, since Kabbalah defines God not as a separate entity but as the fundamental reality of all Being, everything is also God, which means that Torah and God are really just two different modes of the same (every)thing.

Thus, the learning of the Torah in Kabbalah is far more than an intellectual process of studying texts; it is a vital, creative process. On this subject, the Zohar proclaims:

Rabbi Shimon said: Woe to the person who says that Torah presents mere stories and ordinary words! . . . Ah, but all the words of Torah are sublime words, sublime secrets! . . . The stories

*of Torah form only the garment of Torah, and
whosoever thinks that the garment is the real Torah
and not something else—may his spirit deflate!*

As we will see, in Kabbalah the Torah is so much more than texts and words; in essence, Torah is literally an aspect of the Divine. Studying Torah is sometimes described as a romantic or erotic act, both between human and Divine, and within the Divine Him/Herself, similar to eastern Tantra traditions. It's important to be aware that "Torah" can mean any and all of these different things, and its meaning, in any given situation, needs to be determined by context.

THE TANAKH

The Tanakh is the Hebrew Bible. It is an acronym for *Torah* (Teaching, the first five books), *Nevi'im* (Prophets), and *Ketuvim* (Writings). Its narrative begins with the first five books of the Torah, which concludes with the Israelites gathered on the banks of the Jordan preparing to enter the "Promised Land," then continues with the conquering of the land of Canaan in the Book of Joshua.

It tells the story of the first Jewish kings–Saul, David, and Solomon–the building of the first temple, and the eventual corruption of the kingdom that led to its downfall and destruction of the temple at the hands of the Babylonians. The Tanakh tells of the great prophets who preached against this corruption and warned of the calamities that would come to pass, as well as the eventual return from Babylon and the building of the second temple. In addition to this historical narrative, it also contains the Psalms of David, the wisdom books of Solomon, and a few stand-alone stories such as the Books of Ruth and Job.

As mentioned earlier, "Torah" can mean the first five books of the Tanakh, but it can also mean the Tanakh in its entirety. And, just as in Torah, the Tanakh is seen in Kabbalah as merely the outer garment of something much deeper.

For example, in Chronicles 29:11, King David prays:

> To You, God, is the Greatness, the Strength, the Beauty, the Eternity, and the Glory . . .

In Kabbalah, these qualities–Greatness, Strength, Beauty, and so on–signify not mere adjectives of praise, but actual Divine manifestations within the cosmic Kabbalistic glyph, the Tree of Life. We will explore these manifestations, called *sefirot,* later in this chapter, as well as in chapters 2 and 3.

THE MIDRASH

The Midrash, along with the Mishna and the Talmud that we will explore in the coming sections, are the core texts of the early rabbis. But before we dive into them, we need to understand how the rabbis understood Torah in general.

As we have seen, Torah can mean the first five books of the Tanakh, but it can also mean all of the Bible and all of the rabbinic writings as well. This is because, in the view of the rabbis, there are really *two* Torahs: the Written Torah, composed of the five books (or the entire Bible), and the Oral Torah, composed of explanations and interpretations of the Written Torah.

According to tradition, both Torahs were received by Moses on Mt. Sinai after he led the Israelites out of Egypt. Both Torahs were then transmitted in an unbroken chain from Moses to Joshua, from Joshua to the elders, then to the prophets, and eventually to the early rabbis. All the teachings of the rabbis, then, were ultimately a transmission from Sinai, not their own invention.

But how can this be? So many rabbinic writings have to do with matters that were only relevant to their time; not to mention the fact that they often disagree with one another!

The answer is that the Oral Torah is not a fixed text, but a collection of principles: a "spirit of the law" which can take on an infinite number of forms. The rabbinic writings–Midrash, Mishna, and Talmud–were an embodiment or expression of the Oral Torah, which took a written form throughout the early rabbinic period due to concern that the knowledge would be lost if it remained oral.

The first of these major rabbinic writings, the Midrash, is a vast collection of legends (called *midrashim* in the plural, or *midrash* for a singular legend) that fleshes out the Biblical stories of the Torah. For example, let's look at the way the Torah introduces Abraham (whose name was originally Abram):

This is the line of Terah: Terah begot Abram, Nahor, and Haran . . . Abram and Nahor married, the name of Abram's wife being Sarai . . .

GENESIS 11:27-29

Do you notice anything missing? Abram is born in one sentence, and in the next he is getting married! The Torah is often like this, giving only a brief sketch of events. The early rabbis wrote down thousands of stories based on the Torah's characters, usually to teach some particular point.

For example, there's a *midrash* about when Abraham was a child. His father, Terah, was a shopkeeper of a store that sold idols, or statues of deities.

One day, Terah put young Abram in charge of the store while he went out for some errands. Abram took a club and smashed all the idols except for the biggest one. Then, he put the club in the hand of the one big idol that was left.

When his father returned, he was furious: "Abram! What have you done?"

"Father, I didn't do anything! The gods got into a fight and this one smashed all the others!"

"That's impossible!" yelled Terah. "These idols aren't alive!"

"If they're not alive, Father, then why do you worship them?"

Midrashim like this one were an integral part of the tradition by the time Kabbalah emerged, and it was assumed by the authors of Kabbalistic texts that the readers were familiar with them. Many Kabbalistic writings, especially those of the Zohar, were written in the style of the earlier *midrashim*.

THE MISHNA

While the Midrash is composed of legends (*midrashim*) designed to teach lessons, the Mishna is almost entirely composed of short teachings (called *mishnayot* in the plural, *mishna* in the singular) that flesh out Jewish law. Just as in the case of the Torah's brief narratives, the Law of Moses is often brief and ambiguous. The primary function of this rabbinic work, completed around the year 200 CE by Judah the Prince, was to flesh out and clarify the laws of the Torah.

For example, here is a Torah law that seems to be legislating the reciting of the *Sh'ma*, which we looked at earlier:

Sh'ma — Hear Israel, the Divine is your God, the Divine is One . . . You shall speak these words . . . when you lie down and when you rise up . . .

DEUTERONOMY 6:4, 7

This appears to tell us certain times to recite the words beginning with the word *sh'ma* (hear), but it's not clear exactly what times are meant by "when you lie down and when you rise up." If "lying down" means nighttime, can you recite the words any time during the night? When does the night officially begin and end? Let's get a taste of how the Mishna deals with these questions. These are actually the first sentences of the Mishna:

> From what time may one recite the Sh'ma in the evening? From the time that the priests come inside to eat of the sacrifices, until the end of the first watch; these are the words of Rabbi Eliezer.
>
> But, the sages say it may be recited until midnight. Rabban Gamaliel says, until dawn.
>
> Once it happened that Gamaliel's sons came home late from a wedding feast. They said to him, "We have not yet recited the Sh'ma!" He answered them, "If it is not yet dawn, you are still obligated to recite it."
>
> Why then did the sages say "until midnight"? In order to keep a person from accidentally forgetting.

MISHNA, BERAKHOT 1

Mishnayot like this one form the vast majority of the Mishna. They flesh out the often vaguely defined commandments of the Torah into a doable practice, while allowing the reader to follow along with the conversations and logic of the rabbis. In this way, Judaism is not merely a list of *do*s and *don't*s, but a way of thinking. To practice Judaism is to be trained in this uniquely Jewish way of analyzing text.

Both the Midrash and the Mishna supply the literary forms upon which Kabbalistic writings are modeled. Kabbalah also builds on the uniquely Jewish relationship with sacred text and develops it into a transformative practice with cosmic implications, as we will soon explore.

THE TALMUD

Finally, the Talmud is the greatest literary achievement of the early rabbis. The Talmud is a massive work, spanning 63 book-like sections called "tractates." It is structured as a commentary on the Mishna, so the entire Mishna is contained within the Talmud. For example, just as the Mishna begins with the text quoted on page 26 about reciting the *Sh'ma,* the Talmud also begins the same way. Then it goes on for many pages in a stream of consciousness, relating more details about the laws of the *Sh'ma,* as well as anecdotes about rabbinic and Biblical figures similar to the *midrashim,* wisdom teachings, rabbinic debates, and more. A contemporary example of how these texts relate to each other could be similar to how the host of a YouTube video will play a clip from another video, comment on the clip, and then expand further on other topics through a stream-of-consciousness association.

Among the many subjects of the Talmud are some of the earliest descriptions of mystical techniques that were foundational for the later development of Kabbalah. One such technique was called *Ma'aseh Merkavah,* or "Workings of the Chariot." This practice involved creating a kind of astral vehicle through which the soul could leave the body and travel through different worlds. Here's a Talmudic passage that talks about *Ma'aseh Merkavah:*

The Sages taught: An incident occurred involving Rabban Yoḥanan ben Zakkai, who was riding on a donkey and his student, Rabbi Elazar ben Arakh, who was riding a donkey behind him.

Rabbi Elazar said to him, "My teacher, teach me one chapter in the Workings of the Chariot."

Rabban Yoḥanan ben Zakkai alighted from the donkey, wrapped his head in his cloak in a manner of reverence, and sat on a stone under an olive tree.

Rabbi Elazar said to him, "My teacher, for what reason did you alight from the donkey?"

He said, "Is it possible that while we are expounding the Workings of the Chariot, and the Divine Presence is with us, and the ministering angels are accompanying us, that I should ride on a donkey?"

Immediately they began to discuss the Workings of the Chariot and fire descended from heaven, encircled all the trees in the field, and all the trees began reciting song . . .

TALMUD, CHAGIGAH 14B

The Workings of the Chariot formed a genre of mystical literature that also existed separately from the Talmud. Along with the Midrash, Mishna, and Talmud, this early "Chariot" mysticism formed the fertile soil from which Kabbalah was to eventually arise.

THE SEFER YETZIRAH

The Sefer Yetzirah, "Book of Formation," is the first complete Jewish book we have of an overtly mystical nature. Its origin is uncertain; one tradition ascribes its authorship to Abraham, redacted by Rabbi Akiva. By its style, it seems to be an early rabbinic work, as its form is similar to the Mishna.

The Sefer Yetzirah introduces certain Kabbalistic terms for the first time–most notably, the *sefirot*. Later, we will explore the *sefirot* in depth, as they are a foundational concept developed at great length in the Zohar and Lurianic Kabbalah. But in the Sefer Yetzirah, they are simply described as stages in creation, forming a bridge between the Divine and the universe in which we live.

The other central concept in the Sefer Yetzirah is the *otyot*, the 22 Hebrew letters. Both the *sefirot* and the *otyot* are the building blocks of creation, and the letters are expounded in terms of correspondences with astrological symbols, alchemical elements, days of the week, seasons of the year, parts of the body, and more. In this way, the Sefer Yetzirah forms a kind of pre-Kabbalah alternative creation story to the well-known Biblical version.

Here is a taste:

> With 32 mystical paths of Wisdom engraved Yah, the Lord of Hosts, the God of Israel, the Living Divine One, King of the Universe, El Shaddai, Merciful and Gracious, High and Exalted, Dwelling in Eternity, Whose Name is Holy—lofty and holy. He created His universe with three books (Sepharim): With text (Sepher), with number (Sephar), and with communication (Sippur). Ten Sefirot of Nothingness and 22 Foundation Letters (Otyot) . . .

The themes of the *sefirot* and the *otyot* will later become the foundations of two distinct streams within Kabbalah that we will explore shortly. The Sefer Yetzirah is thus foundational for Kabbalah, and continues to be a source of material and inspiration for Jewish mysticism to this day.

THE BAHIR

The Bahir, "Book of Illumination," is the first true text of Kabbalah. The earliest manuscript we have of this medieval mystical work is from 1297, but there are earlier Kabbalistic texts that refer to the Bahir, so there must have been earlier versions. Scholars believe this book originated with a mystical sect in Germany called the *Hasadei Ashkenaz*, the "German Pietists," and eventually made its way to France where it underwent further transformations.

While the Sefer Yetzirah was written in the style of the Mishna, featuring concise, almost technical sounding teachings, the Bahir was written more in the style of the Midrash, quoting Biblical passages and giving them a radically new interpretation in order to teach various Kabbalistic principles in a more narrative-based and homiletic way. It was written mostly in Hebrew, with some Aramaic, similar to the way the *midrashim* were written.

Although the 10 *sefirot* are mentioned in the Sefer Yetzirah, they are mentioned primarily as numbers corresponding to dimensions of space, time, and morality: east, west, north, south, up, down, beginning, end, good, and bad. The Bahir is the first to expand on the meanings of each *sefirah* as Divine emanations and to associate them with the image of a tree, which eventually evolves into the well-known Tree of Life glyph in the Zohar and beyond. The *sefirot* also become associated with the Biblical characters we looked at earlier, as well as particular *middot*—spiritual qualities such as loving-kindness, gratitude, wisdom, and so on. We'll explore all of this later in the book.

Earlier I mentioned the Kabbalistic interpretation of the Biblical creation story in which Adam and Eve are pictured as one androgynous being. This idea is first found in the Bahir, along with the novel Kabbalistic idea that the Divine is both male and female. Here is the opening of the Bahir, in which the first known description of the Divine as overtly feminine appears:

Rabbi Nehuniah ben HaKana said: When the Torah says that Adam was "in the image of God, male and female," it means that the androgynous Adam was created in the form of the

Divine qualities, which too are androgynous. The Hebrew word Tzela, usually translated as "rib," actually should be translated as "side" according to the standard Aramaic translation of the Bible. When the Bible states, "He took one of his ribs," it actually means "one of his sides," that is, the feminine side. The concept of the "Male" is that of giving, while "Female" is that of receiving, holding, and giving birth. Thus, without the Female aspect of God, creation could neither take place nor endure . . .

Unlike the Sefer Yetzirah, which reads like a somewhat technical manual filled with number and letter symbols, the poetry of the Bahir is filled with Eros and sets the stage for the flowering of the Zohar, the ultimate expression of medieval Kabbalah.

THE ZOHAR

Both the Sefer Yetzirah and the Bahir are short, concise works that set the stage for what was to come: the magnum opus of all Kabbalah, the holy Zohar.

When the Zohar appeared, it quickly took its place as the Kabbalistic bible and became the defining text for all Kabbalah that would come afterward.

As mentioned earlier, the man who brought Zohar to the world in the late 13th century was a Castilian Kabbalist named Moses de León. He claimed to have received the text through his secret Kabbalistic channels, and that its true author was Rabbi Shimon bar Yokhai. (Remember him? He's the one who spent 12 years hiding from the Romans in a cave, naked and buried in sand.) According to de León, Rabbi Shimon had channeled the Zohar during his years in that cave.

The Zohar continued to develop several key themes that had already appeared in the Bahir, the most prominent being the concept of the *sefirot* as different aspects or emanations of the Divine. The *sefirot* are unique to Kabbalah, and while the writings about them in the Bahir and Zohar are grounded in both Biblical and rabbinic texts, these writings represent a totally new interpretation of those older texts.

Another theme, connected to that of the *sefirot,* is the idea of masculine and feminine aspects of the Divine. While the idea of God as feminine is, strictly speaking, unique to Kabbalah, there is a Biblical book that comes very close: the Song of Songs of King Solomon.

On the surface, the Song of Songs reads like an erotic love poem, and it might seem out of place in the Bible. The reason it was included, however, is because according to the Midrash and other rabbinic writings, the "maiden" and the "male lover" in the Song of Songs are allegories, representing Israel and God (Israel being the maiden).

The Zohar is profuse with quotes from Song of Songs, but here it takes on a whole new dimension. No longer is the maiden simply a metaphor for Israel, but for *Shekhinah*–the feminine Divine Presence. At the same time, this puts a radical new spin on the connection between Israel and the maiden, which is that it is through our spiritual practice (we being "Israel") that the unification between the feminine and masculine aspects of the Divine is accomplished, along with our own unification with the Divine.

This is the most central and core teaching of the Zohar: that the implication of our mystical quest for returning to Wholeness–our return to the Garden and the Tree of Life reflected in the Genesis story–is accomplished through an erotic courtship between us and the Divine, which is simultaneously a courtship within the Divine Itself.

THE SHULKHAN ARUKH

It may seem out of place to mention the Shulkhan Arukh in a book about Kabbalah. After all, the Shulkhan Arukh is a compendium of Jewish law, and therefore represents the outer, exoteric aspect of Judaism, rather than the inner, esoteric dimension represented by Kabbalah.

However, its author, Joseph Caro, was himself a Kabbalist. In 1646, he produced a work called *Maggid Mesharim*–"Preacher of Righteousness"–which was a kind of mystical diary about how an angel visited him every night for 50 years and taught him the mysteries of Kabbalah, often admonishing him for his shortcomings and instructing him to perform acts of service and asceticism.

While the Shulkhan Arukh is primarily a work of *halakha* (practical Jewish Law), the mystical perspective of the author is present in the very beginning. The book opens by quoting Psalm 16:

I set the Divine before me constantly—Sh'viti Hashem l'negdi tamid.

It then goes on to explain (paraphrased):

. . . for there is no comparison between one who is amongst family or relatives and one who is in the presence of a king. How much more so when you contemplate (that you are in the presence of) the Holy One whose glory fills all creation . . .
. . . as it is said "Do I not fill the heavens and earth?" (Jeremiah 23:24) Bearing this in mind, one will acquire a sense of reverence and surrender before the awesomeness of the Divine . . .

This is essentially an instruction in the mystical practice of *devekut,* which is attaching your awareness to the Divine. In this way, the Shukhan Arukh contextualizes *halakha* as the practical side of Kabbalah right from the beginning, as the daily spiritual practices that express and integrate Divine consciousness.

Let's explore a short exercise to experience *devekut* for yourself.

EVERYDAY KABBALAH

DEVEKUT (ATTACHMENT TO THE DIVINE)
MEDITATION:

Take a few moments to look around, letting your awareness rest in the perception of whatever is present.

As you calmly notice your surroundings, begin to rest your awareness within your body. Feel the flow of your breathing, notice any emotional feelings that might be present, and relax your mind from thinking.

Now bring to mind that everything you perceive—the objects and beings around you, colors and light and sound, the flow of your breath, your emotional tone, the sense of your body in space—all of it is part of one experience, right now.

Notice that all of this is living in the field of your awareness, and that your awareness effortlessly takes the shape of whatever you perceive, but the awareness itself has no shape, no form.

All of this—your awareness and everything perceived in this moment—is simply what is present, all an embodiment of Existence, all an expression of the Divine Presence that is nothing but Reality itself, Existence as it meets your awareness, right now.

In fact, the awareness is not *your* awareness, but it is rather the Divine perceiving through you, in this moment.

Try anchoring this perspective by slowly chanting the words from Psalm 16 that mean "I set the Divine before me constantly."

Sh'veetee Hashem l'negdee tameed . . .

You can return to a state of *devekut* many times throughout the day as you are able. With practice, *devekut* will more and more become your natural state.

Now that we've explored the overarching history of Kabbalah, its major personalities, and its texts, let's dive into the core concepts that underlie Jewish mysticism and give rise to its unique teachings and practices.

CHAPTER TWO

CORE CONCEPTS

T he language and meaning of Judaism unfolds in layers through history. Each new layer that emerges usually seeks to clarify what came before it, while also adding something new. For example, the Mishna sought to clarify the meaning of the laws in the Torah while also adding new laws, and the Talmud sought to clarify the Mishna through new questions and dialogues between the rabbinic personalities quoted there.

Kabbalah, as the inner dimension of the larger reality of Judaism, is also an evolutionary unfolding from its Jewish source texts. Each expression of Kabbalah gives birth to new ideas and continues to evolve to this day. Thus, it would be incomplete to talk about the core concepts of Kabbalah without mentioning the larger garden of Judaism from which they sprang.

For this reason, as we explore these core concepts of Kabbalah, we will simultaneously be visiting their sources in Torah and Judaism.

As we have seen in the last chapter, Kabbalah is, like all spiritual traditions, a response to the basic predicament of humanity: the condition of alienation, of lack, of disunity that gives rise to all the evils and dysfunctions we experience in the world. In this chapter we will explore the deeper questions: How did we get this way? What is the purpose of suffering? What is our basic nature? And, most importantly, what is the map to show us the way back to the Garden, and how can we read it?

THE PURPOSE OF CREATION

In the beginning, God created the heavens and the earth . . .

GENESIS 1:1

When Torah begins its creation story, it neglects to tell us *why* God created the universe. What was God's motivation? On the surface, it might seem that "purpose" is not really a concern of the Torah. The falling of rain and the growing of crops is a concern for the Torah; the continuity of lineage and tribe is a concern; protection from and sometimes the conquering of one's enemies is a concern. But the *purpose of it all* doesn't seem to be a concern; the Torah itself never overtly tells us the reason why anything exists in the first place.

The Kabbalists, on the other hand, were deeply concerned with the question of purpose. The answer for the Kabbalists seems to be hidden in the very next verses:

> God said, "Let there be light," and there was light . . . and God saw that the light was good . . .

GENESIS 1:3, 4

The first thing God creates is light, and then God "sees" that the light is "good." These three concepts–light, seeing, and goodness–become core throughout all teachings of Kabbalah. Different texts express it in different ways, but they basically all come down to this: "Light" is needed for "seeing," so both "light" and "seeing" are actually metaphors for perception, or awareness. Furthermore, God actually *is* the Light; God and the Light are not separate.

The 13th-century Kabbalist Nachmanides points this out in his commentary on the Jewish liturgy, which says God "forms the light and creates the darkness." Only the darkness is created; the light is "formed," implying that the light already existed. And, since nothing was created before light, anything that already existed must not be different from God; hence, the identification of God with the light.

So, "God" and "Light" and awareness are all different ways of saying the same thing, and they all are inherently "good." Here we have our first core concept of Kabbalah, which we might say like this: *The purpose of creation is for awareness to become aware of its own goodness.*

And God created Adam in Its image, in the image of God It created him; male and female It created them.

GENESIS 1:27

Here the Torah describes the creation of human beings "in the image of God." Again, the Kabbalists read into this: Since God is Light and Goodness, then that must also be what we are.

From this developed the idea of the *sefirot* and the Tree of Life. The basic Light/Goodness of the Divine is refracted into 10 different channels, or expressions of Divine energy called *sefirot* (singular is *sefirah*). These *sefirot* can be visually arranged in the shape of both a human being and a tree. This is the Tree of Life and the "image of God" in which humans are created.

The Tree of Life, composed of the 10 *sefirot*, is both a cosmic structure depicting the stages of creation of the universe, as well as our own innermost structure, our Divine nature. When we are aligned with our Divine nature, our inner light can express itself through the *sefirot* as Divine qualities such as love, wisdom, strength, and joy. (We will explore the *sefirot* and their corresponding qualities thoroughly in chapter 3.) In this way, our human existence serves to embody the Divine Light, and God can come to know Itself, through us–*as above, so below*–as the Kabbalistic principle states.

We all have experienced the *middot* in our lives; we know that qualities such as love, joy, and creativity are real because we have experienced them. And yet, we also know their opposite. We experience profound darkness and suffering as well. Kabbalah recognizes this truth of our human existence; it doesn't deny our suffering, but rather places our suffering in context and reveals how we must use it to accomplish our purpose.

In this chapter, we'll explore six core concepts that provide this context: the purpose of suffering; the necessity of desire; the experiential knowing of the Divine; the importance of giving to others and being of service; the reality of free will; and finally, the fruit of the practice, which could be described as spiritual pleasure, or Divine bliss.

SUFFERING

And Hashem God commanded the man, saying, "Of every tree of the garden you are free to eat; but as for the Tree of Knowledge of Good and Bad, you must not eat of it; for as soon as you eat of it, you shall die."

GENESIS 2:16, 17

Adam and Eve have it easy: Everything is good, all their needs are provided for, and they live in a beautiful garden of fruit trees. All they have to do is avoid eating from the Tree of Knowledge of Good and Bad. And yet:

When the woman saw that the tree was good for eating and a delight to the eyes, and that the tree was desirable as a source of wisdom, she took of its fruit and ate. She also gave some to her husband, and he ate. Then the eyes of both of them were opened . . .

GENESIS 3:6, 7

When we were in the womb, everything was good for us, too. All our needs were effortlessly provided for, and problems didn't exist. But there was no awareness of how good we had it; no appreciation of the goodness we were constantly receiving.

And so, in this sense, the goodness wasn't really good; there was no "seeing the Light is good," because there was no contrast. It is only in the world of problems, of struggle, of growing and learning, that we can recognize the good; that's why Adam and Eve's "eyes were opened" when they ate from the Tree of Knowledge of Good and Bad. The word for "knowledge" in Hebrew is *da'at,* which is the same word used to describe sexual union between Adam and Eve, implying that this "knowledge" is not merely intellectual, but experiential.

This is why they ate, even though it brought suffering. They had no choice, just as we have no choice in the womb to be born. Adam and Eve represent consciousness prior to the existence of contrast, and therefore prior to *choice.*

Going back to the purpose of creation, or "the awareness of goodness," consciousness must leave the world of perfection and enter the world of dissatisfaction; it must leave the Eternal Present, and enter the world of time. To appreciate our food, we must work for it; to appreciate this brief moment we are alive, we must live with the knowledge that one day we will die.

"By the sweat of your brow shall you eat bread,
until you return to the ground—for from it you were
taken; for dust you are, and to dust you shall return."

GENESIS 3:19

And so, the fundamental human problem—that of alienation and dissatisfaction leading to all the suffering we inflict on ourselves and each other—is actually the condition through which we may come to fully appreciate Wholeness. And yet, it would appear that we are stuck:

God said to Adam, "Because you ate of the Tree
about which I commanded you, 'You shall not eat
of it,' cursed be the ground because of you; by toil
shall you eat of it." Hashem God banished him
from the garden of Eden, to till the soil from which
he was taken . . . And the cherubim and the fiery
ever-turning sword were stationed east of the
Garden of Eden, to guard the way to the Tree of Life.

GENESIS 4:17, 23, 24

The Divine Wholeness we seek is our own nature; we are created *b'tzelem Elohim,* in the Divine Image, which means that at our core, we *are* Light/Goodness/Consciousness, with the inner structure of the Tree of Life and the *sefirot*. And yet, the "fiery sword" of our thoughts and feelings blocks the way; we are sunk in the world of time, toiling for our bread, doomed to die.

Exile from the Garden of Eden is not the only image in the Torah that tells of this universal human problem. Another major narrative on this theme is the enslavement of the Israelites in Egypt. Just as Adam and Eve had to leave the garden to "toil the ground" in order to "eat bread," so too the Israelites had to descend into Egypt to get their "bread," because of the famine in their land.

But there is also a major difference in the imagery of the two metaphors, adding a more nuanced descriptiveness to our situation. In the case of the Garden, Adam and Eve are driven *out* of the small garden and into the big world. For us, this is being kicked out from the comfort and nourishment of the womb, after which we must *work* to suck milk from a nipple.

But in the case of Egypt, the Israelites left the big world and went into the narrow place. The word for Egypt, *Mitzrayim*, actually means "narrow place."

The smallness of the Garden was like the comfort of a womb, whereas the smallness of Egypt was loss of freedom, the constriction of slavery. For us, the narrowness of Egypt represents the feeling of constriction that comes from the stresses of life and being limited by the relentless boundary of time.

Long after the Torah came into the world, Kabbalah developed its own nuanced narrative of the meaning of suffering. In the system of Isaac Luria, the original *sefirot* shattered because they could not contain the Divine Light that filled them. Shards of these shattered vessels then descended into all physical matter, becoming *klippot*–"husks" within which Divine Light is trapped. These *klippot,* according to Luria, are the source of all evil.

The story of the shattering of the vessels echoes our own experience; just as the original *sefirot* could not contain the Light and shattered, thereby creating evil, so too the womb can no longer contain the baby after a certain point. The process of birth is a traumatic "shattering" of sorts, causing much suffering to the infant right at the beginning of life. Suffering, like the *klippot* of Luria, is the cause of everything we might call "evil." Without the experience of pain and lack, there would be no selfish motivation, and hence no "evil."

Therefore, because suffering is the condition by which we can realize and appreciate essential Wholeness, "evil" is also a necessary condition. And, just as in the redemptive imagery of "returning to the Garden" and "going out from Egypt," Lurianic Kabbalah also describes a process by which the sparks of Light are liberated from the *klippot* within which they are trapped, and *tikkun* ("fixing") is accomplished.

How is this done? How can we free the Light trapped in the *klippot,* get out of Egypt and back to the Garden, and once again eat from the Tree of Life? The process must begin, first of all, with desire.

THE DESIRE FOR SPIRITUALITY

As we have seen, the experience of suffering allows for the recognition of Goodness. This is because, without the experiential contrast between "good" and "bad," between pleasure and pain, there can be no *desire.* Without desire, there can be no receiving of that which is desired, and hence no recognition.

Desire, then, is a fundamental spiritual necessity.

Ordinarily, desire is focused on our natural needs. When we feel hungry, we desire food. When we feel the craving for air, we desire to take a breath. But beyond physical gratification, there is a deeper need. When we begin to sense this deeper need, a genuine desire for spirituality begins to blossom.

This desire is crucial, because spiritual liberation requires a basic change in our worldview, a fundamental shift in the way we relate to our experience, and we won't make the effort to achieve this shift unless we really want it.

MEDITATION:

Bring awareness into connection with your body, with the flow of your breathing, with the feeling of your body's form in space, with any feelings that might be present right now.

Let awareness fill your body, so that it becomes like a vessel filled to the brim with the light of your awareness. Begin chanting these words, which mean "fills all worlds," on a single note or simple melody:

Mimaleh kol almin, mimaleh kol almin . . .

After a few minutes of chanting, shift your focus to become aware of the space around your body. Notice the sounds, the light, the things and beings around you, the shape of the room or the sky and the earth, and the fullness of everything you perceive outside your body.

Next, bring to mind that your perception of everything around you is arising in the field of your awareness, and you are this vast field; your awareness is not merely within your body, but also beyond your body. Your awareness has no shape or form, but takes the form of everything you perceive. And, even as it takes the form of everything you perceive, it is also beyond all form, an openness and aliveness that not only fills everything within your perception but also surrounds it, transcends it.

See if you can sense the vast, open formlessness of your field of awareness, and add the next phrase to the chant, which means "surrounds all worlds":

Mimaleh kol almin, sovev kol almin . . .

Continue repeating this chant for several minutes before coming back to your ordinary activities, refreshed and clear.

What is this fundamental shift?

Ordinarily, we tend to feel that we are a collection of thoughts and feelings trapped inside a body, looking out at a world of separate things and beings. But Kabbalah suggests something different. See how the Zohar describes the Divine in this Aramaic aphorism:

> Mimaleh kol almin u'sovev kol almin—Filling all worlds and surrounding all worlds. . .

ZOHAR III:224A

Or, said in another way:

> Leit atar panui mineha—There is no place devoid of the Divine . . .

TIKKUNEI ZOHAR 57

And in Hasidism, we find this Yiddish statement by Rabbi Yitzhak of Homel:

> Es is mehr nito vie Ehr alein, un vider kehren, altz is Gott—There is nothing but the Divine alone and, once again, all is God.

And in the Torah itself we read:

> The Divine Reality is God in the heavens above and on the Earth below, there is nothing else.

DEUTERONOMY 4:39

In a non-mystical reading of this last text from the Torah, it simply means that there is only one God. But in the Tanya, the classic "bible" of Chabad Hasidism, this is understood to mean that there is *only* God. In other words, God is not a supreme being or supernatural entity, but is rather Existence Itself (as we learned in chapter 1).

Once we make this fundamental shift to seeing all of the elements present right now in our experience as expressions of One Reality, then the nature of our suffering–the "ever-turning flaming sword," the "slavery in Egypt"–also shifts. We see that the feeling of constriction, be it alienation, anger, or any other kind of dis-ease, is itself part of the Divine. The desire you have to get free, to return to the "Garden," is also part of the Divine. And, most importantly, your own consciousness, aware of all these feelings, is also Divine.

When you recognize the simple fact that all things present right now in your experience comprise a Unity, and your awareness itself is also part of this Unity, "Egypt" and the "flaming sword" begin to dissolve on their own, revealing the "Garden" that was there all along.

While there are many spiritual techniques and practices for achieving this transformation, they are all rooted in shifting how we relate to our experience in the present moment.

RECEIVING THE KNOWLEDGE OF GOD

In the story of the Exodus from Egypt, God liberates the Children of Israel with "signs and wonders." In several different places, God tells Moses the reason for these miracles:

I will multiply My signs and wonders ... And the Egyptians shall know that I am the Divine when I bring out the Israelites from their midst.

EXODUS 7:3, 5

In other words, suffering has a purpose, which is to become conscious of the Divine. Our essential self is the "I" in the above quote: "I am the Divine." To get free is to recognize our Divine nature, to receive the true knowledge of God, not as a mere idea or belief, but to know experientially what we are beneath our thoughts and feelings.

This journey of discovery is again expressed in the narrative of the Israelites after they leave Egypt; their destination is Sinai, where they will receive the revelation of Torah that becomes the basis of the entire tradition.

The external content of this revelation consists mostly of the 613 *mitzvot,* or commandments (a singular commandment would be *mitzvah*), the most famous of which are the "10 Commandments." The 10 Commandments are singled out because the Torah depicts their revelation as an almost psychedelic event in which sounds are "seen" rather than heard:

All the people saw the thunder ... and the blare of the horn ...

EXODUS 20:15

While the *mitzvot* served as the guiding laws for ancient Israelite society and later become the basis of spiritual practice as interpreted by the rabbis, the Kabbalists also saw the *mitzvot* as pointing to the realization of the Divinity of all reality.

For example, the first of the 10 Commandments begins:

I am the Divine, your God, who brought you out of the land of Egypt, from the house of bondage . . .

EXODUS 20:2

The first letter of the first word of this first commandment is the letter *aleph*. The *aleph* has an upper point and a lower point, bridged by a line:

According to Hasidic teaching, the upper point represents joy, while the lower point represents bitterness, and the middle line that bridges them is the letter *vav* (ו) which means "and."

When we bring our awareness equally to joy and sorrow, saying "Yes AND" to both pleasure and pain, we go beyond the experience of duality and come to know the underlying Unity of the universe and of our own being. This "Yes AND" attitude is a fundamental aspect of the *devekut* practice that we have been sampling in the meditations throughout this book. We will explore this more in chapter 4.

GIVING

It would be misleading to portray Kabbalists as concerned only with the inner secrets of the *mitzvot*; in fact, much of Kabbalah is devoted to uncovering the practical application of Divine realization through the physical performance of the *mitzvot*.

If mainstream, exoteric Judaism is concerned with external performance, and esoteric, Kabbalistic Judaism is concerned with inner transformation, why are the Kabbalists also concerned with the external stuff–with Jewish laws, rituals, and ethics?

To understand, we must revisit the meaning of the word "Kabbalah." Kabbalah, as we have seen, means "received." On the surface, this refers to the fact that the teachings of Kabbalah were traditionally received by a student directly from the master.

But on a deeper level, "receiving" refers also to the mystical process itself. As we have seen in the story of Eden as well as in our own experience, we begin Whole and Complete, but without knowledge of our Completeness. We have everything we need but aren't consciously aware of what we possess, because we haven't yet experienced its absence. It is only after we lose our Completeness–we get kicked out of Eden, kicked out of the womb–that we can then consciously receive the gift of Wholeness. And, paradoxically, we do that by realizing we never really lost it; it was only covered over by the impressions of external experience, reflected in our thoughts and feelings.

As you may have experienced in the *devekut* meditation exercises, it is not difficult to receive back your Wholeness by simply receiving the fullness of the present moment, acknowledging and embracing its Oneness, and letting yourself fall into that Oneness.

But really *living* that Oneness through all of life, through the bitter, the sweet, and the mundane, requires a life reorientation of *serving* that Oneness. And that's why the *mitzvot* have always been so important to the Kabbalists. The *mitzvot* form a structure of living that is God-centered, that is (if done with the proper *kavanah* or meditative approach) constantly pointing one's awareness back toward the Oneness through one's actions.

Yehuda Ashlag, the great 20th-century Kabbalist and interpreter of Lurianic Kabbalah, explained that the Creator is endlessly giving of Its goodness in the form of Divine Light; the essence of the Creator and the Light is the impulse to give. If we want to make ourselves into vessels that receive this infinite goodness, we must emulate that impulse; we must ourselves become givers. In this way, we form a kind of "circuit" with the Divine Light, and it flows into us effortlessly.

The *mitzvot* are the behavioral aspect of the path, whose purpose is to transform us more and more into "givers" and thereby transform us into vessels for the Light.

While different Kabbalists in different periods have differed somewhat in their views of the *mitzvot*, especially in modern times, the function of the *mitzvot* has always remained an essential aspect of Kabbalah. To realize our Godly essence means to live that Godliness in all our ways, in all our actions, as it says:

In all your ways, know the Divine . . .

PROVERBS 3:6

FREEDOM OF WILL

If you practice this attitude of giving, either with the aid of the *mitzvot* or simply by being of service, you may notice that it is sometimes easy and spontaneous, and other times not so much. Even if we have an authentic desire for spirituality–for leaving our inner suffering behind and getting back to our inner Garden–there seems to be an opposing force within that tempts us back into *Mitzrayim* again and again.

Judaism and Kabbalah have names for these opposing forces. The drive to live from our inner Godliness is called the *yetzer hatov. Yetzer* means "drive" or "impulse" or "desire," and *hatov*

MEDITATION:

Bring to mind a time when you gave your attention fully to someone or something, without any ulterior motive. Perhaps it was listening to a friend tell you something they deeply wanted to share with you. Or perhaps it was seeing the natural wonder of a sunset.

See if you can evoke the inner attitude and feeling of giving your attention in this way: giving from the heart, in the way that you might interact with a baby, or with a beloved animal.

What does that feel like?

Now, see if you can offer your attention to whatever is present in this moment with the same attitude. Don't leave anything out: Notice your body, your breathing, your thoughts as they arise and dissipate, any emotional tone that is present. Notice the space around you, the things and beings that are present with you. Give your attention silently to all of this, opening your heart to be with this moment, as it is.

Spend a few minutes in this silent, present state, with this attitude of giving your awareness from the heart.

---

simply means "good." But we also have the opposite: the *yetzer hara,* the impulse to bad or evil.

Today, we might call the *yetzer hara* the ego. The Tanya has a novel way of explaining this phenomenon. According to the Tanya, we actually have two souls: the *nefesh behamit,* or Animal Soul, and the *nefesh Elokit,* or Divine Soul.

Both of these souls reside in our "heart," the Tanya explains. The Animal Soul is powerful, and its influence tends to rise up from the heart and take over our mind, where it can "clothe itself" in our thoughts, speech, and deeds. Every time we act from a place of anger, craving, or any kind of negativity, it's because the Animal Soul (ego) has taken control.

The Divine Soul resides in both the mind and the heart, so we have the power to prevent the Animal Soul from taking control. We do this by choosing to bring our Divine Soul (awareness) down into the heart, freeing us from the Animal Soul (ego), arousing a profound love in the heart and awakening our inner Godliness.

The Tanya's formulation of the two souls may seem strange, but the technique is fundamental, regardless of whether you use the two-soul language or not. The point is to be aware of the impulses that tend to take possession of your mind. Watch them. Bring the "Divine Soul" down into your "heart" by bringing awareness into your body. Through the concentration of awareness in your body, you can awaken the *middot* (spiritual qualities such as kindness, gratitude, and so on) that arise from the "heart" and choose to live from them, rather than from their opposite. We cannot choose what we feel; our feelings arise as they do. We cannot choose what happens to us; the world unfolds as it does. But we *can* choose how we relate to this moment, and through this power of choice, spiritual transformation can be catalyzed.

ETERNAL PLEASURE

For anyone serious about embarking on this path, it is important to know that it can at times be extremely difficult—not just because the impulses of the *yetzer hara* or Animal Soul or ego (or however you want to label it) are powerful, but because when you decide to be fully present, there will likely be an *increase* in emotional pain before there is a decrease.

That's because our ordinary way of operating is to block ourselves from intense emotional pain, which is totally natural. Pain hurts, so we have inner defense mechanisms to keep it at bay. In the course of life, we encounter plenty of emotional pain, which then gets blocked and trapped in the nervous system.

But, when we begin opening ourselves energetically to be fully present and feel whatever feelings need to be felt, the old pain will eventually surface.

> When Pharaoh does not heed you, I will lay My hand upon Egypt and deliver My ranks, My people the Israelites, from the land of Egypt with extraordinary chastisements . . .
>
> EXODUS 7:6

The famous "plagues of Egypt" that caused tremendous suffering to Pharaoh and the Egyptians hint at this phenomenon: Before the Children of Israel could go out to freedom, there first had to be plagues. Things get worse before they get better. Even after they left Egypt, they complained again and again about Moses and wished they had never left.

When we encounter the inner pain that often precedes spiritual transformation, there are three ways we can avoid getting caught by it.

The first is to remember the big picture. The pain is only temporary; all experiences come and go. The pain is coming up only because it was blocked; once it is felt fully, it will dissipate.

The second is to make joyfulness part of your spiritual practice. Don't be too dire and serious; as the Hasidim taught, serve God with joy!

> Serve the Divine with gladness;
> come into the Presence with glad song!
>
> PSALMS 100:2

This is why singing and dancing have such a central place in Hasidism. We'll explore this more in chapter 4.

Third, remember your goal: the unfolding of your Divine nature. Love *that*; want *that*.

Love Hashem, your own Divinity, with all your heart, all your soul and all your might!

DEUTERONOMY 6:5

Within your inner Garden lies a kind of spiritual bliss that isn't dependent on external factors; it is a bliss inherent within your own being. It is a pleasure brought on not by gratification in time, but by entering the Timeless Present; it is the pleasure of the Eternal.

Now that we have a sense of the journey and goal of the path, let's dive into the core teachings that form the map with which the path is traveled. The teachings we will study are the interface through which the Kabbalist interacts with Torah, Judaism, and life in general. These teachings form a unique, mystical worldview, which offers a way to understand one's own psyche, as well as think about the deeper reality to which the exoteric dimension is believed to point. In other words, these teachings form a language–the language of Kabbalah.

Kabbalah for Beginners

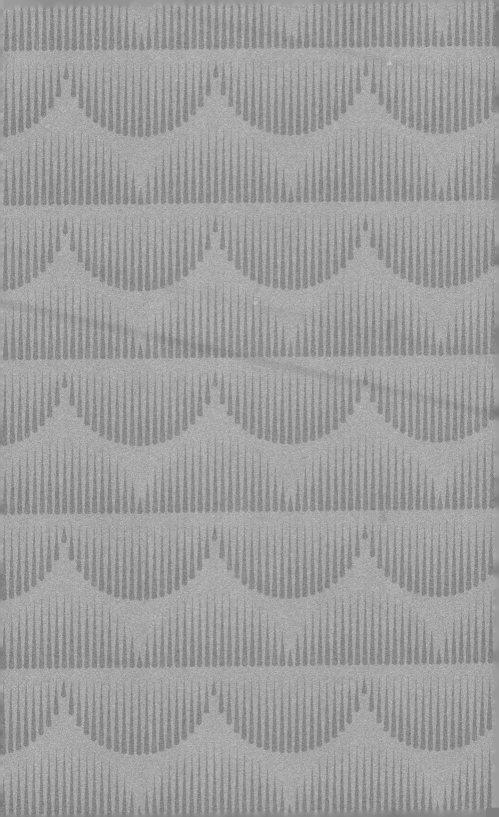

CORE TEACHINGS

efore we dive into the core teachings of Kabbalah, it is important to understand that, like any language, these teachings have evolved over time. The English of Shakespeare is quite different from the English of a New Orleans blues musician. And, if a blues musician who happens to also be a scholar of Shakespeare teaches you English, the kind of English you will learn will likely be a very particular and unique form of English.

My point is, there is no single, true version of Kabbalah; there are many versions that use many of the same words and symbols, yet often with different meanings. Sometimes, the different meanings harmonize well with one another; those that do tend to stick over time and become standard Kabbalistic teachings. Others are more characteristic of only one particular system of Kabbalah.

I will be your Shakespearian Bluesman for this task.

The version of these teachings I will be giving here is not an exhaustive survey of different Kabbalistic symbols and meanings. Rather, I am giving a version that, in my experience, will be most *spiritually useful*. My hope is that you will be able to make good use of these core teachings, and that they will help you build an "inner temple" within which your deepest essence will find a home. Let's dive in.

THE TREE OF LIFE

The Tree of Life, or *Eitz Hayim* in Hebrew, is the central symbol of all Kabbalah. As such, all other Kabbalistic ideas can be related to it. In a sense, the Tree is like a cosmic filing cabinet, each of its parts representing a host of associated realities which together form the whole path. As we saw earlier, the origin of the Tree is the creation story of Genesis at the beginning of both the Torah and the Christian Bible. There, it represents the goal of spiritual aspiration, the source of eternal life and the central feature of the Garden of Eden.

For us, it will be helpful to understand that "eternal life" is itself a symbol—not a magical fountain of youth through which we might live forever in time, but rather a living connection with the Eternal, beyond time, in this present moment.

As we have seen earlier, the Tree is composed of 10 spiritual realities called *sefirot* (singular would be *sefirah*). But the Tree

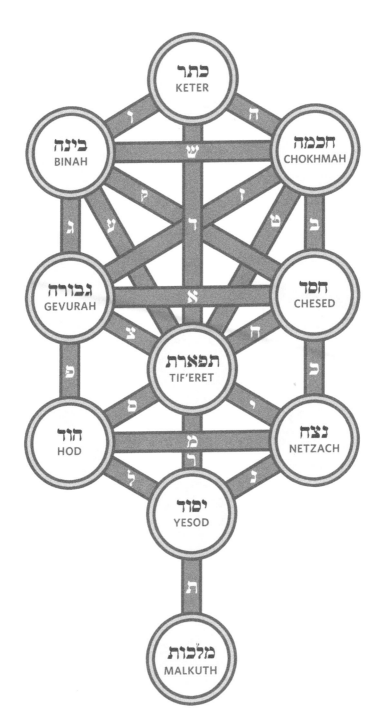

Core Teachings   ∾   61

can also be divided in different ways: nothing and something, worlds, soul levels, and pillars. It is this collection of larger structures that we will explore first.

EYN SOF

Eyn Sof means "without end," "limitless," or "infinite." It describes both the basic quality of reality and the ultimate identity of the Divine. All things exist within the *Eyn Sof,* and nothing can exist outside of It, since It is by definition infinite, eternal, and all-inclusive.

Because It is infinite, It must also include the finite; the Infinite expresses itself as the never-ending stream of finite realities. Thus, we all live within and as the *Eyn Sof;* It is our Source, our Destination, and the Ultimate Identity of our own consciousness. We are, in essence, not separate from the *Eyn Sof* at all.

Furthermore, *Eyn Sof* is not merely an idea, doctrine, or belief. It's true that there are many doctrinal ideas that appear in Kabbalah, but these are beside the point. The true significance of *Eyn Sof* is that It points us to become aware of the deepest dimension of our own experience–the Eternal dimension of the present moment.

That's because, right now, the content of our experience is in constant flux; "right now" never stands still, but changes endlessly. The present moment is *Eyn Sof* by nature, and it is wholly present *in* and *as* our own experience, right now.

Furthermore, all of this flux is happening within something that never changes: the open space of the present moment, which is somehow awake right now *in* and *as* our own awareness. This aspect of *Eyn Sof,* the space of Nothingness within which Somethingness manifests, is called *Ayin.* The ever-changing content of our experience, the never-ending comings and goings of an infinite number of Somethings, is called *Yesh.*

These two aspects of reality form the whole that is *Eyn Sof*, all of which is present right now within our experience of consciousness meeting content, of *Ayin* meeting *Yesh*.

This basic duality of *Yesh* and *Ayin* comprising the Oneness of *Eyn Sof* is represented by the Tree of Life as *Yesh* (Existence), emerging from and within the *Ayin* (Nothingness). Now let's take a look within the Tree Itself in order to see the various ways it can be divided and understood.

FOUR WORLDS, FIVE LEVELS

Experience can be understood, at the most fundamental level, as a unity (*Eyn Sof*) comprised of the duality of awareness meeting form (*Ayin* meeting *Yesh*). Furthermore, within the *Yesh*—within all of which we are aware—we can discern three more aspects: sensory awareness, feeling or mood, and thought.

These four dimensions of experience, the *Ayin* of awareness itself and the *Yesh* of sensory awareness, mood, and thought, are understood in Kabbalah to be the "Four Worlds." These "Four Worlds" also correspond to the four letters of the Divine Name mentioned in chapter 1, transliterated as Y-H-V-H.

Another way of looking at these dimensions of experience is in terms of levels of the soul. Soul levels and worlds aren't really so different from each other; they are internal and external ways of looking at the same thing. For example, when you see a tree, there is the *seeing* of the tree, which would be the "soul level" of sensory awareness, and then there is the *tree itself*, which belongs to the "world" of physical things.

Let's look at each of these soul levels, along with the worlds in which they live, and learn the Kabbalistic terms for them.

The soul level of sensory awareness is our perception of the physical. This soul level itself divides into different senses, such as seeing, hearing, tasting, and so on. Sensations are also included in this soul level: hot and cold, pleasure and pain, salty and sweet, and so on.

The world in which all these physical phenomena exist is called *Olam Asiyah*, the "World of Action." The soul level that lives in *Asiyah* is called the *nefesh*. The word *nefesh* can also mean "soul" or "person" in ordinary, non-Kabbalistic Hebrew.

The soul level of emotion and feeling encompasses the tone or mood of life and lies somewhere between the physical and the mental. Our feelings influence the kinds of thoughts that arise, and through our conscious choosing of which thoughts we think and which thoughts we release, we can influence what kinds of feelings we experience. Feelings are reflected in our physical bodies, and every emotion has its correlate of hormones, neurotransmitters, immune responses, and so on. Generally speaking, positive feelings are healthy for the body.

The world in which emotions and feelings exist is called *Olam Yetzirah*, the "World of Formation." The soul level that lives in *Yetzirah* is called the *ruakh*. In a non-Kabbalistic context, *ruakh* means both "spirit" and "wind," hence its association with emotion. In common usage, *ruakh* can mean energy or enthusiasm, as in, "That music has a lot of *ruakh*."

The soul level of thought encompasses all mental activity, from the automatic understanding of words in our spoken language, to deliberate problem solving, to the unintentional meanderings of the mind. The world in which thought lives is called *Olam Briah*, the "World of Creation." This soul level of thought lives in *Briah* and is called the *neshamah*. The word neshamah is very close to the word *nishmah*, which means "breath." *Neshamah* is often used in ordinary Hebrew to mean soul in general and is usually used in a more intimate and affectionate way than *nefesh*, as in, "She is a good *neshamah*."

Beyond these three soul levels is a less commonly known fourth level, associated with the *will to be*. This soul level is called *hayah*, which means "livingness," referring to the basic impulse to live and exist. The world within which *hayah* dwells is called *Olam Atzilut,* or the "World of Origin."

Beyond *Atzilut* and beyond the *will to be* of the *hayah* is the *Ayin* Itself, the Nothingness, corresponding to the soul level *yekhidah*. *Yekhidah* means "unique" and "one-of-a-kind," because there is really only one *yekhidah*. *Yekhidah* is the pure awareness beyond all will and beyond all qualities. It is the same in all living beings, though it can express itself in an infinite number of ways.

These four worlds–*Asiyah, Yetzirah, Briah, Atzilut,* and the *Ayin* beyond them–together with the five soul levels of *nefesh, ruakh, neshamah, hayah,* and *yekhidah,* comprise this next level of the Kabbalistic map of consciousness and reality. From here, we can further divide these five into the 10 *sefirot*. But before we do, let's look at the basic dynamic through which the 10 *sefirot* manifest.

THE THREE PILLARS

In one of the most common depictions of the *sefirot* on the Tree of Life, they are seen along three columns, with three *sefirot* on the right, three *sefirot* on the left, and four in the middle. These three columns, known as the Three Pillars, represent a dynamic and dialectical relationship through which the *sefirot* interact and counterbalance one another.

The Right Pillar is generally seen as masculine, giving, and expansive. The Left Pillar is seen as feminine, receiving, and restrictive. These simple dualities then manifest through more specific qualities of each *sefirah,* which is why it is good to understand this dynamic first, before getting into the meaning of each *sefirah* separately.

The Middle Pillar is the resolution between the right and left, pointing the way toward harmony by balancing opposing qualities such as masculine and feminine, giving and receiving, and expansive and restrictive. In this sense, the symbolic teaching of the Three Pillars is incredibly practical and applicable to an infinite number of life situations and activities.

For example, we can apply the teaching of harmonizing right and left in the practice of meditation itself:

On the right side, meditation involves *giving* your awareness to whatever is present, unconditionally and unreservedly. This has an expansive quality to it, because as the mind clears and awareness connects with what is present, the open quality of awareness becomes reflected and felt on the *ruakh* and *nefesh* levels–the levels of feeling and sensation–as bliss and relaxation.

At the same time, in order to sustain this expansiveness, it is necessary to *restrict* the thinking mind at the *neshamah* level, noticing and letting go of thoughts as they arise. It is also helpful to restrictively direct awareness into the body, bringing it all the way down to the *nefesh* level. Paradoxically, when awareness leaves the higher realm of *neshamah* (thinking) and comes all the way down to *nefesh* (physical sensation), it simultaneously reveals the *hayah* and *yekhidah* levels, creating a sense of identity with spacious awareness rather than with the physical body alone.

Thus, restrictiveness leads to expansiveness; giving leads to receiving. If we want to live a life that is balanced and harmonious, we should learn to apply these basic dynamics of the Three Pillars to all of life's situations.

Now, let's look at the *sefirot* themselves and see how this dynamic expresses itself through them.

THE 10 SEFIROT

The 10 *sefirot* (note: *sefirot* is plural, *sefirah* is singular) are a more detailed elaboration of the five levels of the soul and the four worlds. The first *sefirah* is identical to the world of *Atzilut* (Origin); it is the first emergence of consciousness out of the *Ayin*, within which the simple *will to be* arises. Its equivalent in the personal dimension is the soul level of *hayah*, which is simple awareness. (The highest soul level, *yekhidah*, corresponds to the *Ayin*, or Nothingness, from which the Tree is born.)

The next two *sefirot* both encompass the world of *Briah* (Creation), which is the world of thought. This world corresponds in the personal dimension to the soul level of *neshamah*, which is the thinking mind. The next six *sefirot* correspond to the world *Yetzirah* (Formation); they represent the basic feeling-states and attitude qualities (*middot*) corresponding to the soul level of *ruakh*, the emotions. The final, 10th *sefirah* corresponds to the world of *Asiyah* (Action), representing the physical world. The soul level is *nefesh*, which is sensory awareness.

Let's now go through each *sefirah* in more depth, as well as explore the relationships that arise between them.

KETER: THE DIVINE CROWN

The designation of *Keter* as the Divine Crown invokes the image of a king/queen and expresses the idea that humans are created *b'tzelem Elohim*, "in the Divine image." The Tree of Life is itself both an abstract image of a human form, as well as a diagram of the inner dynamics of God. The "crown" of God is the basic *will to be* discussed earlier, corresponding to the world of *Atzilut* and the soul level of *hayah*.

We needn't understand this *will to be* literally; rather, we should understand that, just as we have a basic impulse to live and stay alive, the universe also has an impulse toward existing. As we saw in chapter 1, existence itself is understood as inherently good—*God saw that the light was good*—and "good" simply means that which is desired.

This is a circular argument, connecting with another meaning of *Keter,* which is "circle." In fact, its meaning as "crown" is derived from its meaning as "circle." This circularity hints at the idea of *Keter* as essentially unknowable: that *Keter* is beyond all logic and understanding. In other words, *it just is.*

Keter, then, is the first manifestation of *Yesh* (Something) from *Ayin* (Nothingness) as the basic impulse to be. At this level, the *Yesh* is not *being anything* in particular yet; it is simply an *impulse* to be, which also implies *be*coming. Accordingly, the Divine Name that is generally associated with *Keter* is *Ehyeh Asher Ehyeh,* which can mean both "I Will Be What I Will Be" as well as "I Am That I Am," Being and Becoming in One.

This Name, *Ehyeh Asher Ehyeh,* is the Name that God gives Moses at the burning bush. In the story, Moses is a Hebrew who was raised as an Egyptian in Pharaoh's palace. At this point in the story, he is living the life of a simple shepherd after running away from his conflicted life in Egypt. He sees a strange sight—a bush that burns but is not consumed—so he goes to investigate. God then speaks to him from the bush and tells him he must go and lead the Children of Israel to freedom. Moses protests a few times, then asks God how he should answer when they ask who sent him. God responds with this Name: *Ehyeh Asher Ehyeh.*

The hint here is that the impulse to exist, the *will to be,* is linked to freedom, which as we have seen is linked to goodness. They are all different modes of the same thing; the infinite

MEDITATION:

Bring your awareness to the top of your head; you can touch the crown of your head with your hand if it helps focus your attention there. If you are able, imagine the letter aleph above your head:

Aleph is the first letter of the Hebrew alphabet, and represents *Keter*, the first *sefirah*, which is the Divine Crown and original impulse to be.

Imagine a stream of light descending from above, through the top of your head, around and through your body, and down into the earth. Let the light fill you with the ecstasy of simply being; feel the Divine Light of creation as your own life energy in your body. This is the light of *Keter*, emanating from the world of *Atzilut*, within which lives your soul level of *hayah*.

Now, use your right hand to cup the right side of your skull, and bring to mind the vast field of consciousness within which all your perceptions are happening right now. This is *Hokhmah*, from the world of *Briah*, within which your soul level called *neshamah* lives.

Bring your left hand to cup the left side of your skull as well, and take a few moments to be aware of the rising and falling thoughts in your mind. This is *Binah,* also from the world of *Briah* and your soul level of *neshamah.*

Now bring your right hand to your heart and feel a light from your heart shining out and filling your body. Take a few moments to feel whatever emotion or feeling is present. What does it feel like? Whatever feelings are present, know that they belong to the world of *Yetzirah,* within which lives your soul level of *ruakh.*

Finally, with your right hand on your heart, bring your left hand to your belly. Take a few moments to fill the organs in your belly with awareness, then let the awareness expand and spread down through your legs and toes; upward to fill your chest; down through your arms and hands and fingers; and upward once again into your head, skull, brain, face, and facial muscles. Be aware of your physical form and the feeling of your body. Notice your senses: sound, sight, smell. Know that this belongs to the world of *Asiyah* within which lives your soul level of *nefesh.*

Spend some time in connection with *Asiyah,* the world of sensory awareness, resting awareness on your breathing, and letting go of thoughts as they arise. After some time, come back to your ordinary activities refreshed and renewed.

non-being, *Ayin,* expresses its essential freedom by *becoming,* for the sake of the essential goodness of *being.* Realizing this freedom and goodness is the essence and goal of Kabbalah. We can practice this by being aware of the miraculous and incomprehensible gift of being and by acting from the motivation to serve the Source of this gift.

This is *Keter*: the first expression of creation, the most fundamental Something that arises first from the Nothing, the impulse toward the Goodness of Being.

HOKHMAH: WISDOM

The second *sefirah* is called *Hokhmah,* which means "wisdom."
As we have seen, *Keter* is the *will to be* inherent in consciousness, and in order to *be* there must also be *becoming. Keter,*
then, is the first creative impulse. *Hokhmah* is the first *expression* of this impulse–the arising of thought within the field of
awareness.

You can experience *Hokhmah* right now. Just be still and
notice what thought arises in your mind next. Where did the
thought come from? If you inquire into the workings of your
own mind, you will see that thought arises in the mind spontaneously; it is a direct experience of *Yesh me'Ayin*–"Something
from Nothing"–that is constantly happening.

People who are creative in their work or hobbies intuitively
know about this process. They may have no experience
with meditation, but when they need a fresh, creative idea,
they will become still and allow the idea to emerge. From a
Kabbalistic point of view, this would be understood as the
practice of activating one's inner *Hokhamah,* and moving from
the thinking mind into the vast space of consciousness from
which thoughts spontaneously and creatively flash forth.

Next, we move from the origin of thought in *Hokhmah* to the
process of thinking itself.

BINAH: UNDERSTANDING

While *Hokhmah* is the source of thought, the flash of insight
within the field of awareness, *Binah* is the development of
thought, the actual activity of thinking.

It is especially important in meditation to learn to differ-
entiate between *Hokhmah* and *Binah,* to discern between
the *arising of thought* and the *thinking of thought*. The arising
of thought happens spontaneously, and we can't directly

control it. We can, however, choose whether or not to engage with the thought once it has arisen; we can choose to either develop the thought through the process of thinking or simply let the thought dissipate and fall back into its source, the field of consciousness called *Hokhmah*.

When we choose to restrict our thinking by not engaging with thoughts as they arise, this leads to the experience of expansiveness, the feeling of the vastness of consciousness, the *Hokhmah* within which thought arises. On the other hand, when we *do* engage with thinking and thereby move into *Binah*, there can be an experience of constricted-ness, of getting "absorbed in your head." Thus, we have the first example of the Three Pillars in action: *Hokhmah* is expansiveness, the right side, and *Binah* is limitation, the left side.

Right and left are seen mythically as masculine and feminine, and this is reflected in the personification of *Hokhmah* and *Binah* as the supreme *Abba* and *Imma*, the Divine Father and Mother. These images also have a sexual and reproductive dimension, as *Hokhmah* is sometimes pictured as gushing forth with water, while *Binah* is the great womb of all creation.

Our exploration of *Binah* completes the first triad of the Tree, with *Keter* at the top of the Middle Pillar, the original impulse of creation to be and become, *Hokhmah* on the right as the expansiveness of consciousness within which thought spontaneously arises, and *Binah* on the left as the constricting of consciousness into the act of thinking.

HESED: MERCY

As we move to the *sefirah* of *Hesed*, we move also from the world of Creation to the world of Formation: the realm of emotions and mood called *Yetzirah*. The world of *Yetzirah* encompasses the next six *sefirot*, which are linked with particular attitude-qualities called *middot*. Each *middah* is also linked to a Biblical character believed to embody each quality.

Hesed is the quality of loving-kindness, and is seen as the most fundamental and important *middah*. It is a bit of a paradox, because you would think that the most fundamental quality would be in the center column of the Tree, yet *Hesed* is on the right side of the Tree, counterbalanced by *Gevurah* (Strength) on the left. And while it is, on one hand, the balance of right and left that is seen as the ideal harmonious relationship within the Tree, emphasizing *Hesed* is also seen as ideal.

A way to understand this paradox is that the Middle Pillar— the balance of right and left—is ideal in the *practical* sense, but this balance is actually for the *sake* of loving-kindness. In other words, in order for loving-kindness to actually be loving and kind, it has to be balanced with strictness, restraint, and limitation.

Think of how we interact with children. If you really love a child, you want to *give* to them; giving is an expression of love. But suppose the child wants to run out into the street? If we give them permission, our "love" will likely lead to disaster. Of course, we must say no; we must sometimes *appear* to them as if we are being mean and unloving *for the sake* of love.

Another example would be the case of spoiling a child. *Hesed* wants to say "yes" to everything, but we know that would lead not to satisfaction, only to ever-growing demands. We need the "no," not because "no" is good in itself, but because the "no" is *for the sake* of "yes."

From this point of view, we can see how *Hesed* is the root and purpose of all the *middot,* yet it is simultaneously one side of a polarity. From a value point of view, *Hesed* is the center; love is the center. But from a practical point of view, *Hesed* is on the right and must be balanced by the left; love must be balanced by judgment, "yes" by "no."

In the Zohar, *Hesed* is associated with the patriarch Abraham. Abraham is the archetype of hospitality, as depicted here in this Biblical passage:

> Looking up, Abraham saw three men standing near him. As soon as he saw them, he ran from the entrance of the tent to greet them and, bowing to the ground, he said, "My lords, if it please you, do not go on past your servant. Let a little water be brought; bathe your feet and recline under the tree, and let me fetch a morsel of bread that you may refresh yourselves . . ."

GENESIS 18:2-5

Abraham also exemplifies *Hesed* in his service to the Divine. In one example, he leaves his home and everything familiar to settle where God points him. In another example, he is even willing to sacrifice his beloved son, Isaac.

> God put Abraham to the test. He said to him, "Abraham," and he answered, "Here I am." And He said, "Take your son, your special one, Isaac, whom you love, and go to the land of Moriah, and offer him there as a burnt offering on one of the heights that I will point out to you."

GENESIS 22:1-2

The story of the "binding of Isaac" may seem strange as a *Hesed* story. Abraham, the archetype of loving-kindness, is about to slaughter his own child?

But we must remember that child sacrifice was a common practice in the ancient Near East. To offer your child to the gods was an act of supreme sacrifice and devotion. Unthinkable today, but that's the point; Abraham was willing to surrender his child, but then God stops him:

> Abraham picked up the knife to slay his son. Then an angel of the Divine called to him from heaven: "Abraham! Do not raise your hand against the boy, or do anything to him. For now I know that you fear God, since you have not withheld your son, your favored one, from Me."

GENESIS 22:10-12

Abraham proves his loving-kindness toward God, but then God commands a deeper loving-kindness: *Do not raise your hand against the boy*! Thus, in a world where child sacrifice was commonplace, Abraham's relationship with the Divine signifies the end of this ghastly practice for the Hebrews, and the beginning of a new level of loving-kindness coming into the world.

GEVURAH: STRENGTH

On the other hand, Isaac, as the one about to be sacrificed, came to be associated with *Gevurah* (Strength), sometimes called *Din* (Judgment). The image is that of Isaac bound on the altar, experiencing the ultimate judgment from God as he waits to be slaughtered by his father. Thank God, it was only a test! But the fact that he had to confront his own death at the hands of his father associates him with this fiery counterpoint to *Hesed*.

While *Hesed* represents love, service, and saying "yes," *Gevurah* represents restraint, limitation, and saying "no." As a spiritual life principle, *Gevurah* is associated with asceticism; rather than fulfilling our desires whenever they arise, we can purposefully restrict our gratification in order to increase our freedom from desire. This is the principle behind fasting and *kashrut*, the restrictive eating practices of Judaism.

While Judaism is not a particularly ascetic path, self-restraint is a necessary principle in any spiritual system. Here is an example of how this "left-pillar" principle is expressed in the wisdom text, Pirkei Avot, which appears in the Mishna:

> Such is the way of Torah: you shall eat bread with salt, and rationed water shall you drink; you shall sleep on the ground, you shall live a life of restriction, and in Torah shall you labor. If you do this, "Happy shall you be and it shall be good for you" (Psalms 128:2): "Happy shall you be" in this world, "and it shall be good for you" in the world to come.

PIRKEI AVOT 6:4

Later in Pirkei Avot, it says that Torah is acquired through 48 qualities, among which are "limited pleasure, limited sleep, and limited laughter."

Again, it's important to know that these qualities aren't goals in themselves. But as expressions of *Gevurah*, they serve to correct the corrupting tendency of unbridled *Hesed*. The ideal is for *Hesed* and *Gevurah* to be in balance, which then gives rise to a third *sefirah* that unifies them.

TIFERET: BEAUTY

The sixth *sefirah* on the Tree of Life is the integration of *Hesed* and *Gevurah*. It appears on the Middle Pillar of the Tree directly below them, forming a synthesis from the thesis of *Hesed* on the right, and the antithesis of *Gevurah* on the left. It is called *Tiferet*, which can mean "beauty," "splendor," or "grace." It is also sometimes called *Rakhamim*, which means "compassion," giving the triad another nuance of *Hesed* as "reward" and *Gevurah* as "punishment," with "compassion" lying somewhere between them.

Just as *Hesed* and *Gevurah* are associated with the first two patriarchs, so *Tiferet* is associated with the third patriarch, Jacob, also known as Israel. These two names, Jacob and Israel, indicate his uniqueness, in that Jacob goes through the most pronounced personal transformation out of the three patriarchs.

The name Jacob means "heel" because he is the second born of twins, and he comes out holding the heel of his brother Esau. Esau grows up as a hunter, but Jacob "dwells in tents."

One day, Esau comes in from the hunt empty-handed and asks Jacob for some stew. Jacob demands that Esau sell him his birthright for the bowl of stew, which he does. Later, when their father Isaac wishes to give Esau the blessing of the firstborn, Jacob pretends to be Esau at the urging of their mother and steals Esau's blessing. Thus, Jacob embodies his name, acting as a "heel" toward his brother twice by acquiring both his birthright and blessing.

Much later, after many hardships, Jacob goes to confront his brother, who wants to kill him. Jacob sends gifts to Esau to appease him, then spends the night wrestling with a mysterious being, traditionally considered to be an angel. Jacob is victorious, and as dawn approaches, the angel asks to be released. Jacob tells the being he must bless him first, to which the being replies:

"Your name shall no longer be Jacob, but Israel, for you have striven with God (sarita-El) and human, and you have prevailed."

GENESIS 32:29

The name Israel is derived from *sarita-El,* which means "strives for God." When Jacob (now Israel) finally confronts his brother, Esau forgives him. They hug and kiss and make peace. Jacob has overcome his fear and his selfishness. He has "striven for Godliness" and is transformed.

In an alternative way of attributing Biblical characters to the *sefirot,* Jacob and Esau sometimes represent *Hesed* and *Gevurah:*

Jacob works for his uncle Laban for many years, embodying the service quality of *Hesed.* He is also pictured twice as preparing food. He prepares the stew for Esau, and later he prepares a dish for their father, embodying the giving quality of the right side of the Tree.

Esau, on the other hand, is a hunter and a trapper, skilled with a bow and arrow. He also vows to murder his brother, all *Gevurah* qualities.

Until the transformational moment, Jacob and Esau are in opposition to each other. Just as in the example of how *Hesed* would spoil children without the help of *Gevurah,* so too Jacob is like a spoiled child until he reconciles with Esau. But when they do reconcile, he becomes Israel, the "God-man," the splendorous integration of *Hesed* and *Gevurah* as *Tiferet*.

Accordingly, *Tiferet* represents the persona of God, the actual deity whose "right hand" is Mercy (*Hesed*) and whose "left hand" is Strength (*Gevurah*). In this way, the abstract symbol of the Tree of Life serves as a Kabbalistic elaboration on the more simple, concrete, and mythic image of God in the Bible.

NETZAKH: ETERNITY

The seventh *sefirah* is *Netzakh,* which can mean "victory" or "eternity." Its *middah* (spiritual quality) is persistence, the quality of aiming for a goal and never giving up. Accordingly, the Biblical character for *Netzakh* is Moses, who tirelessly led the Children of Israel for 40 years through unfathomable hardships. In one passage, Moses is pictured as sitting and hearing the problems of the Israelites all day long, until his father-in-law chastises him and tells him to appoint other leaders to help with the burden.

> *The next day, Moses sat as magistrate among the people, while the people stood about Moses from morning until evening. But when Moses' father-in-law saw how much he had to do for the people, he said, "What is this thing that you are doing?" Moses replied, "It is because the people come to me to inquire of God." But Moses' father-in-law said to him, "The thing you are doing is not right; you will surely wear yourself out, and these people as well. For the task is too heavy for you; you cannot do it alone . . ."*

EXODUS 18:13-18

In terms of spiritual practice, the dual meanings of *Netzakh* as "victory" and "eternity," as well as the *middah* of persistence, describe both what we need on the path to succeed, as well as the goal: One must have ruthless persistence in order to gain victory over one's ego and break through to the eternal dimension of experience, the inner freedom of the vast "wilderness" of awareness itself, transcending all slavery in the "Egypt" of ego.

HOD: GLORY

On the flipside of *Netzakh*, we have the eighth *sefirah* called *Hod*, which can mean "glory" but also "gratitude" and "humility." *Hod* is the antithesis of *Netzakh*, just as *Gevurah* is the antithesis of *Hesed*, and serves to correct for the potentially dangerous potential of too much *Netzakh*.

What is too much *Netzakh*? Since *Netzakh* represents relentless persistence to reach a goal, its shadow side would be impatience, a lack of ability to just be with things as they are. The forward-moving, future-oriented energy of *Netzakh* is necessary to break through inertia and transform, but to really be helpful it must be counterbalanced by gratitude for having come to this moment and for being as we are, and humility to know that things will unfold as they should; we don't have to "push too hard."

Accordingly, the Biblical character associated with *Hod* is Moses' brother, Aaron. According to tradition, Aaron was a skilled peacemaker. While Moses was the lawgiver, demanding high standards of the Children of Israel, Aaron employed psychology to soften the hearts of enemies and help them reconcile.

One *midrash* describes the way Aaron would deal with people in a dispute: He would go to each of them separately and tell them the other was very sorry and wanted to make peace, only they were too embarrassed to do so. In this way, each would forgive the other and they would reconcile. Accordingly, we find this rabbinic aphorism:

Hillel used to say: be of the disciples of Aaron, loving peace and pursuing peace, loving people and drawing them close to the Torah.

PIRKEI AVOT 1:12

Just as Moses and Aaron embodied the dual qualities necessary to lead the Israelites, so too *Netzakh* and *Hod* are the essential ingredients for spiritual growth, aiming upward at the archetypal transformation of Israel represented by *Tiferet*.

YESOD: FOUNDATION

The ninth *sefirah* is *Yesod*, which means "foundation." Out of all the *sefirot*, the name of this one is perhaps the least descriptive, probably because of the body part associated with it.

As indicated earlier, *Hesed* and *Gevurah* are the right and left hands of both God and the human form. *Tiferet* is the chest or heart, hinting at its quality of *rakhamim*, compassion. *Netzakh* and *Hod* are the right and left legs. And, in classical Kabbalah, *Yesod* is the reproductive organ–in particular, the penis, whose "seed" is the generative impulse of all creation.

Accordingly, *Yesod* is associated with joy, pleasure, connection, *Eros*, and creativity. This is also perhaps why it is called "Foundation." Without joy, none of the *middot* of the other *sefirot* will last for long. If our spiritual work is to bear fruit, it has to be enjoyable and done with joy. Joy is the fuel that keeps love and discipline alive, and gives us the energy and the heartfulness to persist.

The Biblical archetype for *Yesod* is Israel's favorite son, Joseph. Joseph had perhaps the most difficult life out of any of the Biblical figures; he was almost murdered, then sold into slavery by his jealous brothers. He was then thrown into a dungeon for a crime he didn't commit: He was falsely accused of raping his master's wife after she attempted to seduce him and he resisted. This is another reason for the association of Joseph with the reproductive organ. But, unlike the potentially destructive side of male sexual energy, this is the circumcised organ: the sign of the Covenant of the Jewish people with God. For this reason, Joseph and *Yesod* are called *HaTzaddik*, the "Righteous One," because Joseph was able to resist temptation, thus representing a refined sexual energy that is used only for good.

Through all of his travail, Joseph never complained once, and eventually he rose up to become royalty in Egypt, second in power only to Pharaoh. He didn't get bogged down; like cream, he always rose to the top.

Similarly, if we want to succeed spiritually, we will also need this foundational ability to enjoy the juiciness of life, to not be thwarted by disappointment, and to turn ever toward the positive. As the psalm says,

> Serve God with joy; come into the Presence with glad song!

PSALMS 100:2

As the last *sefirah* of the third triad, *Yesod* is a synthesis of *Netzakh* and *Hod* before it. It embodies the Moses quality of persistence, while staying humble and accepting the moment as it is like Aaron. In the classical image of the Tree of Life, it also serves as the single connecting link between all the preceding *sefirot* with the 10th and final *sefirah*; in this sense as well, it is the "foundation" upon which the Tree rests and transmits its flow into the world.

MALKHUT: KINGDOM

The 10th and final *sefirah* is called *Malkhut,* which means "kingdom." Metaphysically speaking, *Malkhut* is the spiritual energy that gives rise to the physical world. In the experiential sense, *Malkhut* is the world of *Asiyah,* the world of the senses, and the soul level that lives in this world is the *nefesh.*

Malkhut is a particularly feminine symbol, representing *Shekhinah:* the indwelling feminine Divine Presence. As we discussed in chapter 1, it is the courting and ultimate unification of *Shekhinah* (represented by *Malkhut*) with *Kudsha Brikh Hu,* the "Blessed Holy One" (the masculine aspect of the Divine represented by *Tiferet*), that is the aim of the Kabbalah. This Divine "romance" is seen as a cosmic process through which the ultimate *tikkun* (fixing) will take place to bring about the messianic era, but also as an individual process that happens within the Kabbalist.

In a practical and direct way, we can experience this "unification" any moment by bringing our awareness (*Kudsha Brikh Hu,* masculine) to the *content* of our awareness (*Shekhinah,* feminine). In other words, we bring about this "romance" within reality when we become fully present.

The *middah* associated with *Malkhut* is the quality of trust–of knowing and appreciating the great mystery at the root of all being, "breathing" us and everything into existence in this moment. The messianic era is pictured as a time when this awareness will be universal, and the world will truly become the "Kingdom of God." Accordingly, the Biblical figure associated with *Malkhut* is King David who, according to legend, is the progenitor of the Messiah.

MEDITATION:

Take a moment to notice your surroundings, perceiving the things and beings in your space. Bring to mind that everything you perceive is a form of Divinity; all are manifestations of the One.

Next, bring to mind that the awareness with which you perceive everything is also the Divine, as aware as you, right now. Know that when you bring your awareness from within yourself into connection with whatever you perceive outside yourself, it is actually God connecting to Itself.

Spend some time making this intimate connection, allowing this Divine wedding to take place through you. Chant these words, which mean "For the sake of the unification of the Blessed Holy One with the *Shekhinah,* the Divine Presence . . ."

L'shem yikhud Kudshah Brikh Hu U'Shekhintei . . .

Spend some time chanting and connecting before moving back into your ordinary activities.

MAPPING KABBALAH: A SUMMARY

Up to this point, we have looked at both the context of Kabbalah through its core concepts, as well as the map of Kabbalah through its core teachings. Let's briefly recap:

Reality is, at its deepest level, Divine; there is an inherent "Goodness" and "Wholeness" from which the universe springs. This basic goodness is called "Light" and this Light manifests as our own awareness. The impulse of consciousness is to know its own Goodness, and so the universe comes into existence in order to give rise to conscious beings through which this can happen.

We, as conscious beings, are embodiments of this Light/Goodness/Wholeness. We are *b'tzelem Elohim*, the "Image of the Divine."

But, in order for us to become aware of our Divine essence and appreciate the Light, we must first enter into the worldly life of polarities: pleasure and pain, good and bad, love and hate. Our task is to become more and more conscious so that we can "wake up" from these polarities, recognize our Divine essence, and live that essence in the world. In this way, we effect *tikkun*; we forge a unity within God's own Being by forging a unity within our own being.

This is the context, woven from the core concepts of Kabbalah.

In order to bring about this *tikkun* and fulfill the purpose of our existence, we need two things: a map of the path and the tools with which to walk the path.

The map is the *Eitz Hayim*, the Tree of Life. The Tree shows us the qualities that we need to cultivate, and the tools are the means by which we do the cultivation. The qualities are: Will/Intention (*Keter*), Creativity (*Hokhmah*), Focused Thinking (*Binah*), Loving-Kindness (*Hesed*), Self-Restraint (*Gevurah*), Presence (*Tiferet*), Persistence (*Netzakh*), Gratitude/Humility (*Hod*), Joy (*Yesod*), and Trust (*Malkhut*).

These teachings map out the transformational process we will undergo on our journey.

In the next chapter, we will begin to explore the practices themselves, and the tools through which transformation comes about.

CHAPTER
FOUR

PRACTICES, TRADITIONS, AND RITUALS

T he traditional practices of Kabbalah are, as mentioned earlier, the *mitzvot:* actions prescribed in the Torah as Divinely given "commandments." According to tradition, there are 613 *mitzvot* in the Torah. These were later developed by the rabbis into thousands of laws and customs. Despite this complexity, they can be classified very simply and universally into three main categories, as expressed in Pirkei Avot:

Shimon the Righteous was among the survivors of the Great Assembly. He used to say, "Upon three things the world stands: Torah (learning), Avodah (prayer, meditation, and ritual), and Gemilut Hasadim (acts of kindness)."

PIRKEI AVOT 1:2

Torah means "study," referring to the mental or conceptual dimension. *Avodah* literally means "work" or "service" and refers to what we tend to think of as the spiritual practices of prayer and meditation, encompassing the experiential dimension. *Gemilut Hasadim,* "acts of loving-kindness," are the social dimension in which the other two find expression. We will begin by looking broadly at these three categories, and then we will get into some of the specifics through an exploration of the way sacred time is practiced in the holy days of Judaism.

THE STUDY OF HOLY TEACHINGS

The above Pirkei Avot text talks about three categories of practice, not merely as the foundation of a spiritual life, but as the foundation of the entire world. One way to understand this is through the rabbinic teaching that every person is an entire world, because every person has the potential to "give birth" to infinite offspring through our deeds (as well as biological reproduction). But on a deeper level, if we take to heart the principle that the Divine purpose of existence is fulfilled through us, then the foundations of the spiritual path are in fact the foundations of the world as well.

In order for any spiritual path to be successful, it needs to work on all the different aspects of our being. While there are an infinite number of ways to divide a person, Shimon's three-part structure is elegant and useful: Torah (learning) works on our thinking; *Avodah* (spiritual practice) works on how we experience reality; and *Gemilut Hasadim* (acts of loving-kindness) are how we express the teaching in our lives with other beings.

Torah comes first, because all deliberate action begins with thought. Even activities that are entirely physical depend on the inner structure of thought for support, or they won't endure. In sports, for example, we have coaches who give "pep talks." These talks program the thinking of the athlete to support the incredible effort they will have to make.

It is also worth noting that while Torah is primarily an activity of thought, it is not merely intellectual. It is also a creative process through which new insight is generated, and in Kabbalah, it is even an erotic process.

See how words of Torah are described in this *mishna:*

Rabbi Halafta of Kefar Hanania said: When 10 sit together and occupy themselves with Torah, the Shekhinah abides among them, as it is said: "God stands in the congregation of the Divine." (Psalms 82) . . . How do we know that the same is true even of one? As it is said: "In every place where I cause My Name to be repeated, I will come unto you and bless you." (Exodus 20:21)

PIRKEI AVOT 3:6

Practices, Traditions, and Rituals ൭ 89

Here we see that the study of Torah is not merely an absorbing of information; there is an experiential sense of the Divine that becomes present when one engages in the process.

Another important feature of Torah learning is that it is not aimed at any particular endpoint. Rather, it is a life practice to be engaged in every day, like exercise. In this way, the nervous system is constantly growing–new neurons forming and new connections being made–like an inner Tree of Life, nourished by the waters of sacred text.

PRAYER

Ordinarily, we tend to think of prayer in a dualistic way, as the words of a human addressing the Divine. From a psychological point of view, this is true; it is through the imagining of God as an entity whom we address that prayerfulness is achieved. But at the same time, Kabbalah conceives of the Divine not as an entity, but as Being Itself. The great Tree of Life, symbolizing both All Existence as well as our own inner structure, is not believed to be created by an external deity; rather, the deity emerges from the dynamics of the *sefirot*. The myriad forces, the *Elohim*, are all part of a Unity that fills and transcends everything.

This was expressed simply but profoundly by the Hasidic master, Rabbi Pinchas of Koretz:

> The prayer that a person says is itself God. It is not like when you talk to your friend; your friend and your words are two different things. It is not so for prayer, for the prayer, you who are praying, and God, are all One.

If this is so, then why is prayer conceived of in a dualistic way?

Part of the answer is in the word for prayer. The verb "to pray" in Hebrew is *mitpalel*. This is a reflexive verb, meaning one who prays acts upon oneself. All Hebrew words come from three-letter roots; *mitpalel* comes from the root *Pei-Lamed-Lamed*, which means "to clarify" or "decide." In other words, the aim of prayer is to recognize and bring forth the deepest essence of our being: the "Light" of all creation, the Wholeness and Goodness within. To bring forth this Light from within ourselves is to become prayerful. We do this by speaking to that Light, and we are aided in our speaking by imagining that Light as a separate deity. At the same time, however, we can understand that the Divine is not separate. We can hold both perspectives at once so as not to take either one too literally. In this way, the cultivation of relationship with the Light through prayer becomes the means through which prayerfulness is achieved.

There are three kinds of prayer–praise, thanksgiving, and petitioning–which are expressions of awe, gratitude, and desire.

Praise is about making ourselves sensitive to the great mystery of everything, bringing ourselves to a state of awe for the wonder and majesty of it all. Praise is impersonal, in that it brings us out of our personal concerns and into awareness of the vastness beyond.

The glorious majesty of Your splendor and Your wondrous acts will I recite . . .

PSALMS 145:5

Gratitude has a similar energy, but here it is personal; we bring to mind the innumerable blessings and ways in which we are supported in this moment. Here is a prayer to be said as soon as one wakes up in the morning:

I give thanks before You . . . for You have mercifully restored my soul within me . . .

Petitioning expresses our desires:

Grant us today and every day grace and kindness and mercy in Your eyes and in the eyes of all who see us!

Petitioning may seem strange if we do not understand God to be a separate entity. But through expressing our desires prayerfully, they are set free from ego and our ordinary identification with them. To truly pray our desires to God is to surrender them, to put them in God's hands, so that our consciousness bound within them is set free. In this way, desire with prayerfulness becomes the means to freedom from desire.

ACTS OF LOVING-KINDNESS

The final foundation of Shimon's three-part formula is called *Gemilut Hasadim*, "acts of loving-kindness." Just as *Hesed* (loving-kindness) is seen as the root of all the spiritual qualities, so too is the practice of kindness toward people and creatures seen as the root of all spiritual action.

There's a story in the Talmud (Shabbat 31a) about the first-century sage Hillel. One day, a man approached him and said that he wanted to convert to Judaism, but only if Hillel could teach him the entire Torah while "standing on one foot."

Hillel replied, "Whatever is hateful to you, don't do to others. That is the whole Torah. The rest is explanation of this. Now go and study it!"

EVERYDAY KABBALAH

TORAH AND AVODAH:

Be in a place where you can meditate undisturbed. Take a few conscious breaths, then begin reading this excerpt from Psalm 27, letting yourself dwell on any part to which you feel drawn.

As you read, keep in mind these questions: What do these words remind you of? Do they resonate with anything in your experience? Do they give rise to any questions? Let yourself contemplate freely for several minutes.

PSALMS 27:

The Divine is my light and my help; whom shall I fear? The Divine is the stronghold of my life; whom shall I dread? When evil men assail me to devour my flesh—it is they, my foes and my enemies, who stumble and fall. Should an army besiege me, my heart would have no fear; should war beset me, still would I be confident.

One thing I ask of the Divine, only this do I seek: to live in the house of the Divine all the days of my life, to gaze upon the beauty of the Divine, to meditate in Its Sanctuary.

Select a verse or verses that are particularly emotionally resonant for you, that seem to express something you feel or have felt. Try reading these passages again out loud or in your heart, but this time, read them as prayer. Try to read them not as something external to you that you are exploring, but express the words from your heart.

If you're not used to praying in this way, it may take some time before you feel comfortable. But, if you stick with it, you will find your way to prayerfulness. Prayer is, as Rabbi Pinchas said, the Divine speaking through you. As you learn to express words of prayer from your heart, you will also come to experience the words themselves as Divine.

Hillel's understanding of Torah as an expression of kindness is shown in the Torah itself in the supreme *mitzvah*:

You shall love your neighbor as you love yourself.

LEVITICUS 19:18

This *mitzvah* is foundational not only because it is the basis of ethics, but because it completes the purpose of creation. Remember that, according to Kabbalah, the universe comes into being so that the inherent Wholeness and Goodness of the Divine Light can be perceived. Furthermore, we are *b'tzelem Elohim*, the "image of the Divine," meaning our consciousness is also that Light/Goodness/Wholeness; we discover the Divine as the root of our own being.

Therefore, to uncover our own Divine nature is to discover our own desire to bestow goodness, and this is expressed in our actions toward others. Others, in turn, are also *b'tzelem Elohim*, so our actions toward others are also actions toward the Divine. This connects the *mitzvah* of "love your neighbor" to another *mitzvah*:

You shall love Hashem, your own Divinity, with all your heart, all your soul and all your might . . .

DEUTERONOMY 6:5

These two *mitzvot*, "love your neighbor" and "love the Divine," are different ways of approaching the same thing: connecting with our own deepest nature, seeing that Divine Light in everyone and everything, and expressing that awareness in action.

There's a story that a disciple of the Hasidic master Rabbi Shmelke of Nikolsburg asked, "We are commanded to love our neighbor as ourselves. How can I do this, if my neighbor has wronged me in some way?"

"You must love them as something which you yourself are," replied the *rebbe*. "All souls are one. They are all sparks from the original soul of Adam. If your right hand accidentally cut your left hand with a knife, would you then go and cut your right hand as punishment? It is the same with your neighbor."

"But master," the disciple went on, "if someone is evil, how can I love them?"

"You know that every person is a spark of the Divine. If one of those sparks forgot its essence, wouldn't you have mercy on this Divine spark that has become lost?"

In this Hasidic story we have the essential unity between loving God and loving people. It may not seem at all obvious how to do this, just as with the disciple in this story, but the *rebbe* reminds us to reframe our experience so that we can wake up to the Divine essence in all beings.

OBSERVANCE OF HOLY DAYS

Now that we have a sense of the broad categories of spiritual practice as *Torah, Avodah,* and *Gemilut Hasadim,* let's explore the specific practices of the Jewish holy days. The holy days serve as interfaces with the Divine qualities (*middot*) embodied in the *sefirot.*

Why do we need interfaces?

Nowadays, we're all familiar with computers. But most of us have no experience with how they actually work. Instead, we use some kind of interface; we see icons on a screen, and we point at the images and click.

Similarly, the great spiritual traditions use cultural practices as interfaces for the spiritual dimension. The most common of these "interfaces" is the observance of sacred times, or holy days. Each of the Jewish holy days is seen in Kabbalah as the embodiment of a specific set of spiritual qualities, and the observance of the holy day connects the celebrant with those qualities.

Through the repetition of the rituals, songs, teachings, and prayers of the weekly, monthly, and yearly holy days, the connection is strengthened, and these "interfaces" allow the *middot* to work on the individual and the community in ever deeper levels.

SHABBAT

Shabbat comes from the Hebrew root which means "to rest" or "to dwell." *Shabbat* first appears in the Torah's creation story, in which God creates the universe in six days and rests on the seventh. The next mention of it comes in the book of Exodus, when Moses tells the Israelites not to collect food on the seventh day because God has given them the seventh day as *Shabbat,* a holy day of rest.

In the Exodus story, Moses has just led the Israelites from slavery in Egypt to freedom. In that context, it appears as a kind of Labor Day: a sacred affirmation of their freedom and devotion to the Divine power that freed them.

In Kabbalah, however, *Shabbat* is much more than a day of rest. Earlier we discussed how Kabbalah sees God as composed of both masculine and feminine qualities, and that the spiritual purpose of creation–the realization of the inherent goodness of Being as the Divine Light embodied in our own awareness–can be pictured as the uniting of the masculine and feminine aspects of God.

Shabbat is the consummation of this idea; it is a kind of cosmic wedding between *Kudsha Brikh Hu* (The Blessed Holy One) and *Shekhinah* (The Divine Presence). And, like a wedding, *Shabbat* has a tone of ecstasy and joy that is reflected in its rituals.

For example, the central hymn for welcoming *Shabbat* on Friday night, written by the 16th-century Kabbalist Rabbi Shlomo HaLevi Alkabetz, is called *"Lekha Dodi"* or "Come My Beloved," and describes *Shabbat* as a Divine bride. At the climax of the hymn, the doors are opened and *Shabbat* is welcomed into the room where she is believed to unite with the masculine or transcendent aspect of the Divine. This is why, for traditional Jewish couples, Friday night is seen as the ideal time for sexual intimacy; physical intimacy becomes an outward expression of Divine intimacy.

On an experiential level, as the nervous system rests from mundane concerns and relaxes into the simple pleasures of eating, drinking, or sexual intimacy, consciousness is set free on *Shabbat* to taste the bliss and joy of simply being. In this way, the rituals and customs of *Shabbat* allow every celebrant to taste a bit of the *oneg*–the joy of being–regardless of how experienced or knowledgeable one is with spirituality. The context of observing *Shabbat* is itself powerful enough to elicit this experience in anyone who is open.

ROSH HODESH

Rosh Hodesh is the celebration of the new moon. *Rosh* means "head" or "beginning" and *hodesh* means "moon" or "month." Judaism has its own unique calendar in which the months are based on the actual moon cycles. However, it differs from other lunar calendars in that it contains "leap months" every few years in order to keep each month in its particular season. This way, the annual holidays that fall on a particular day of a particular month will stay within their appointed seasons (as they do in our Gregorian calendar, which is solar).

Like *Shabbat*, *Rosh Hodesh* has a particularly feminine quality. Just as fertility waxes and wanes in a monthly cycle, so too Israel, with her assents and descents throughout history, is symbolized by the waxing and waning moon. As we have seen, the first instance of Israel being characterized as feminine is in the Song of Songs book of the Bible, an erotic love poem. According to the sages, the maiden is an allegory for Israel, and her lover is an allegory for God. The Song of Songs is replete with the imagery of renewal and springtime, of flowers and trees.

Rosh Hodesh, as the day of the new moon, likewise represents this quality of renewal–particularly the renewal of our soul, our spiritual connection with our essence, and the Divine essence of all. The observance of *Rosh Hodesh* is expressed mostly in the particular prayers and psalms that are unique to it. In some communities, a festive meal is eaten, and some light candles. Jews will greet each other, "*Hodesh Tov!* Good month!" In modern times, *Rosh Hodesh* has become a time for women to gather, and many uniquely female-centered rituals have come into practice.

ROSH HASHANAH

Rosh Hashanah is the Jewish New Year, and it usually occurs sometime during September. As before, *rosh* means "head" or "beginning" and *ha-shanah* means "the year." Strangely though, unlike our Gregorian New Year, *Rosh Hashanah* is the first day of the *seventh* month, not the first month. The reason for this is that there are actually *four* different new years in the Jewish calendar. *Rosh Hashanah* is the New Year for humans and for counting the years. Other "new year" days mark the new year for calculating the reigns of kings, which is on the first of the first month; the new year for the trees; and the new year for the ancient animal tithes.

Rosh Hashanah is the masculine counterpoint to the feminine *Rosh Hodesh*. Its main theme is the coronation of God, and the prayers of *Rosh Hashanah* express the celebrant's deliberate acceptance of God as "King." The main ritual of *Rosh Hashanah* is the sounding of the *shofar*, an instrument made from a ram's horn and played a bit like a bugle. The *shofar* is sounded 100 times on *Rosh Hashanah,* with particular sound combinations that have mystical significance.

On the inner level, the "coronation of God" represents the turning (*teshuvah*) of our hearts and minds toward our Divine Source and Essence, and away from ego and wrongdoing. In this spirit, the major themes of *Rosh Hashanah* are acknowledging one's past misdeeds, asking forgiveness, forgiving others, and reaffirming and renewing one's commitment to the spiritual path.

YOM KIPPUR

Yom Kippur is the Day of Atonement. *Yom* means "day" and *kippur* means "atonement." Both *Yom Kippur* and *Rosh Hashanah* are called the *Yamim Nora'im,* the "High Holy Days," since together they embody the process of renewing the year through our *teshuvah* (turning again toward the Divine, forgiveness, getting back on track). The 10 days after *Rosh Hashanah* are known as the Days of Repentance, culminating in *Yom Kippur. Yom Kippur* is observed with a full 25-hour fast: no food or water for an entire day and night. The prayers are characterized by asking God for forgiveness, and the practice during this time is for people to ask forgiveness from one another.

In the original *Yom Kippur* rites when the temple stood in Jerusalem, the High Priest would enter the *Kodesh HaKodashim,* the "Holy of Holies," which was the inner sanctum of the sanctuary that would only be entered by the High Priest one day of the year. There he would offer incense and pronounce the otherwise unpronounceable Divine Name, mentioned earlier, which means "Being" or "Existence." (This was the only time and the only person who was allowed to pronounce this

Name.) Through the High Priest's special rituals, atonement would be granted for the whole nation.

Although the temple no longer stands and this ritual is no longer performed, the liturgy and energy of the day evokes that sense of intimacy with the Divine and aids the celebrant in opening up on a deeper level and entering the "Holy of Holies" of one's own heart.

SUKKOT

Sukkot means "shelters," referring to the temporary hut-like structures that the Israelites built at certain points in the wilderness during their Exodus from Egypt. (*Sukkot* is plural; a singular shelter is a *sukkah*.) This seven-day holiday commemorates that journey of the Exodus and comes as a festive resolution to the more serious High Holy Days of *Rosh Hashanah* and *Yom Kippur.*

The holiday of *Sukkot* is ritually remarkable in its practice: Celebrants build temporary structures outside the house—in the yard or courtyard or on the roof—and dwell in these *sukkot* for the entire seven days of the holiday, spending time and eating meals within their shelter. The *sukkah,* with its openness to guests and the elements, with a roof made of foliage, embodies the transience and temporariness of life and makes it into a celebration of the fragile present.

For each of the seven days, a special invocation is intoned for inviting in one of the seven *sefirotic* figures: Abraham for *Hesed* on the first day, Isaac for *Gevurah* on the second, and so on. In this way, the seven days become a way to connect with the seven lower *sefirot* and their energies through the *mitzvah* of hospitality. This is also a time to invite friends, family, and community into the *sukkah,* along with the invoked Biblical archetypes. Today, many have added the four matriarchs and other female

Biblical figures to invoke the seven *sefirot,* and some celebrants will invite the spirits of deceased ancestors as well.

The other major ritual of *Sukkot* involves waving a ritual bundle composed of three specific plants, plus a citrus fruit similar to a lemon, in the six directions. The three plants are myrtle, willow, and a palm frond, which together are called the *lulav.* The citrus is called an *etrog,* or citron. These four species represent the four letters of the Divine Name mentioned earlier, transliterated as Y-H-V-H. Thus, the *lulav* and *etrog,* which come from four different trees representing the four letters and thus the four worlds, are symbols of the Tree of Life Itself. Waving them in the six directions is a ritual to invoke universal blessing and channel that blessing into the world.

On an inner level, the holding together of the "four species" (as they are called) in one's hands and waving them in the six directions together represents the 10 *sefirot.* The ritual aims at bringing together the four dimensions of our experience (sensory, feeling/mood, thought, and awareness) into a unity within ourselves, and dedicating our inner unity toward service and blessing for all.

EVERYDAY KABBALAH

One thing nearly all the holy days have in common is the eating of festive meals (with the exception of *Yom Kippur,* which is a fast day). Jewish holy days always begin at night. Accordingly, the evening meal that begins the holiday is much more than dinner; it is a sacramental ritual whose symbolic elements serve to shift the consciousness of its participants and sanctify the transition into sacred time, which really means a dropping away of time and a blossoming of presence.

In a traditional Jewish home, this sanctification is experienced every week on Friday night, as the beginning of *Shabbat*.

Try this:

Prepare a special meal to serve and gather with other like-minded friends or family for a *Shabbat* meal on Friday night. Have ready two candles, matches or a lighter, a cup of wine, a vessel for pouring water over the hands with a big bowl to receive the water, two loaves of *hallah* or some other bread covered with a cloth, and some salt.

Begin the evening by lighting the candles. Gesture with your hands to "wave" the light of the candles into yourself, then cover your eyes with your hands and chant the blessing:

Barukh Atah Adonai Eloheinu Melekh HaOlam, Asher Kid'shanu B'mitzvotav Vitzivanu L'hadlik Ner Shel Shabbat. (All respond: *Amein*)

Gather around the table and begin the meal by inviting everyone to express some gratitude or offer a blessing. Then, lift the cup of wine and chant the blessing:

Barukh Atah Adonai Eloheinu Melekh HaOlam, Borei P'ri Hagafen. (All respond: *Amein*)

Drink the wine and share wine with others.

Next, everyone pours water over each of their hands three times. This is a ritual of purification done before eating bread, for the purpose of washing away the concerns of time so that you may enter fully into communion with the Divine Presence.

Finally, uncover the loaves of bread, lift them up, and chant the blessing:

Barukh Atah Adonai Eloheinu Melekh HaOlam, Hamotzi lekhem min ha'aretz. (All respond: *Amein*)

Sprinkle some salt on the bread. Break the bread and distribute, then enjoy the meal. This is *Shabbat*!

SHEMINI ATZERET

Shemini Atzeret comes the day after *Sukkot* ends, giving *Sukkot* the feeling of an eight-day festival. *Shemini* actually means "eighth" and *atzeret* means "assembly," so it's the sacred assembly that happens on the eighth day after the seven days of *Sukkot*.

Shemini Atzeret is unique among all the holidays in that it has very little meaning associated with it. All of the other holidays have special rituals and stories, like the ones mentioned above and the ones we will look at in the coming pages. But *Shemini Atzeret* is different. The Torah describes it like this:

> The eighth day shall be a sacred time for you. You shall bring a fire offering to the Divine; it is a gathering (atzeret); you shall not work at your occupations.
>
> LEVITICUS 23:36

Such a holiday without the meaning of stories and the richness of special rituals may seem boring. But from a mystical point of view, this absence of content is actually the deepest content! Representing the *Ayin* (Nothingness) from which everything is born, *Shemini Atzeret* is about Presence, pure and simple. The 11th-century rabbi and prolific commentator known as Rashi cites a parable to explain this quality of *Shemini Atzeret*:

> Once there was a king who proclaimed a festival for seven days. All of the kingdom attended, along with the king's family. When the seven days were over and all the people went home, he asked his children to stay just a little longer . . .

The idea is that, while *Sukkot* is a universal holiday about bringing blessing to all the world through the ritual of the *lulav* and *etrog, Shemini Atzeret* is about just being with the Divine for Its own sake, like a father spending time with his children.

SIMKHAT TORAH

As if eight days weren't enough, in the diaspora (dispersion of the Jewish people outside the land of Israel), a ninth day is added: *Simkhat Torah.*

In fact, an extra day was added to many of the Jewish holidays for when they are practiced outside the land of Israel. The original reason for this was that in ancient times, there might be confusion about which was the correct day, so the extra day helped ensure that at least one of the two days would be correct. But the Kabbalists saw a deeper significance to the two days; they believed that the spiritual energy of the holy day would take more time to be absorbed outside the Jewish homeland. For this reason, two days are still observed, even though we don't have the problem of not knowing which day is correct anymore.

So, *Simkhat Torah* is not really a separate holiday from *Shemini Atzeret,* but since *Shemini Atzeret* is called "eighth" (*Shemini*), and since it is almost devoid of any particular meaning, the second day of *Shemini Atzeret* was given some meaning: a celebration of the Torah itself.

The reason for this meaning is that the Torah is read in a yearly cycle, one portion per week. *Rosh Hashanah,* as the beginning of the year, is the time when the Torah cycle nears the end, after which the reading cycle returns again to the beginning. On *Simkhat Torah,* the very last words of the Torah are read and then the Torah immediately starts over with the words, *"In the beginning of God's creating the heavens and the earth . . ."*

As the culmination of the High Holy Days and *Sukkot, Simkhat Torah* is an incredibly festive holiday, with lots of singing and circle dancing with the Torah, often accompanied by drinking alcohol. In Israel, *Shemini Atzeret* and *Simkhat Torah* are celebrated as the same day.

HANUKKAH

Hanukkah, which means "dedication," is perhaps one of the most widely known Jewish holidays in the Western world because it comes around Christmastime. *Hanukkah* is actually one of two minor festivals. In Kabbalah, however, *Hanukkah* powerfully embodies the very core of the teaching that the Divine "Light," the Goodness and Wholeness of Existence, miraculously reveals itself as the essence of our own consciousness if we *dedicate* ourselves to awakening It.

Ironically, the origin of both *Hanukkah* and Christmas is probably the same: a pagan festival on the 25th of the winter month now called December, celebrating the "rebirth of the sun" around the time of the winter solstice. For Christians, this was recast as Christmas, celebrating not the birth of the "sun," but of the "son."

Hanukkah also comes on the 25th, not of December but of the Hebrew month of *Kislev.* It recounts events recorded in the Book of Maccabees which took place during the second temple period in the 2nd century BCE. According to this book (ironically preserved today in the Christian Bible rather than the Jewish Tanakh), a group of Jewish rebels known as the Maccabees defeated the imperial Seleucids (Syrian Greeks) who had defiled the Temple and made Jewish practice illegal. According to the Talmud, when they attempted to rededicate the Temple by lighting the sacred seven-branched lamp called the *menorah,* there was only enough oil for the lamp to burn for one day. But a miracle occurred and the *menorah* burned for eight days, until more oil could be produced.

In Kabbalah, oil is a metaphor for consciousness, and the burning of the oil for light represents that quality of our awareness to "burn away" separation and "enlighten" us to recognize the Divine nature of ourselves and all reality. Furthermore, *Hanukkah* is observed for eight days, and the number eight represents infinity and transcendence of time.

The message of the *Hanukkah* miracle is that the reward we receive from our practice far exceeds the time and energy we put into it. The main ritual of *Hanukkah* involves lighting a *menorah*-like candelabra called a *hanukia* for each of the eight nights of the festival, along with eating special festive foods fried in oil.

PURIM

Together with *Hanukkah*, *Purim* is the second of the two minor festivals, and like *Hanukkah*, it commemorates events that happened long after the receiving of the Torah on Sinai. Also like *Hanukkah*, it seems to have its roots in an earlier pagan festival: in this case, a springtime festival of revelry, upon which the Christian Mardi Gras may also be based.

Purim celebrates the story recorded in the Book of Esther in the Bible, during the time of the Babylonian exile, right after the destruction of the first temple. It tells how the wicked Haman, advisor to the Persian king Ahasuerus, convinced the King to murder all the Jews in the kingdom. Haman had been incensed by the insolence of the Jew Mordechai who refused to bow down to Haman in the street, and because of this, he plotted to have all the Jews killed.

But, unbeknownst to both Haman and the King, the King's wife Esther was a Jew herself, and the niece of Mordechai. Mordechai convinced Esther to risk her life by pleading on behalf of the Jews to the King. She was successful, the Jews were saved, and the evil Haman was hung on the gallows.

Interestingly, the Book of Esther is the only book in the Hebrew Bible which does not mention the Name of God. And yet, the story unfolds with much coincidence, with the various characters being in just the right place at the right time to bring about the happy ending.

Kabbalists and Hasidic masters interpreted this to express that the Divine is hidden in all things, invisibly ever-present. Just as in the serendipitous events of the story, so too are all things unfolding according to the unseen Divine wisdom beneath the surface.

From this point of view, then, *Purim* is about trust, letting go, and surrendering into the hands of the Divine. It is about understanding that beneath the duality of good and bad there is a unity, an underlying goodness with no opposite.

Accordingly, the celebration of *Purim* (like Mardi Gras) traditionally includes intoxication and masks. The Talmud says that one should become so intoxicated that one can no longer tell the difference between "Blessed be Mordechai" and "Cursed be Haman." It is also traditional to dress in costumes and masks, hinting that the whole world is actually the "costume" or "mask" of the Divine. The mood of this festival is joy, as the Talmud says about the month of *Adar* in which *Purim* takes place, "When *Adar* enters, joy increases!"

PESAKH (PASSOVER)

Pesakh, Passover, is perhaps the most foundational of all Jewish holidays because it celebrates both the origin of the Jewish people, as well as the deeper and more universal process of spiritual freedom. The central rite of *Pesakh* is a ritual meal called a *seder. Seder* means "order," referring to the fixed order of steps in the ritual.

The *seder* recounts the Exodus from Egypt through storytelling and ritual reenactment. Some of the major features of this rite are four cups of wine symbolizing four stages of liberation; four questions that are designed to stimulate conversation; the eating of "bitter herbs" as a symbol for the bitterness of slavery; and, most famously, the eating of *matzah*, unleavened flatbread which represents the haste with which the Children of Israel had to leave Egypt. (The bread is unleavened because, according to the Torah, there was no time for the dough to rise.)

The word *Pesakh*, "Passover," refers to the final of the 10 plagues against the Egyptians: The angel of death caused all the firstborn in Egypt to die, but it "passed over" the houses of the Hebrews and left their firstborns to live.

While *Pesakh* has always been a holiday of celebrating and reinforcing Jewish identity, it also has a universal mystical element. For example, in Kabbalah, the unleavened *matzah* represents freedom from ego. Ordinary bread is fermented with yeast, which causes the dough to rise by making tiny bubbles. These bubbles cause the dough to separate from itself. In a similar way, when our egos "puff up," we too get separated from our true essence. According to this understanding, the eating of *matzah* is a ritual for collapsing the ego and entering into an intimate and direct relationship with Reality. In this way, we too go out from our bondage to our limited and constricted sense of self (represented by Pharaoh and Egypt), and into the vast "wilderness" of Reality, in which we meet our Divine essence.

COUNTING THE OMER

The Torah says that the Children of Israel should count 49 days between *Pesakh,* the holiday of the Exodus, and *Shavuot,* the holiday of the Giving of the Torah on Mt. Sinai:

You shall count seven weeks for yourself; you shall begin to count seven weeks from the time you begin to put the sickle to the standing grain. Then you shall celebrate Shavuot to Hashem your God with a tribute of a freewill offering of your hand, which you shall give . . .

DEUTERONOMY 16:9-10

An *Omer* is a measure of grain, like a sheaf. The springtime and early summer festivals of *Pesakh* and *Shavuot,* with their emphasis on offerings of grain, clearly relate to the agricultural cycles and probably originate from earlier pagan agrarian festivals. In the Bible, they take on new meaning related to the historical experience of the Jewish people, and with the Kabbalists, the mystical dimension emerges.

In Kabbalah, the 49 days of the counting of the *Omer* came to represent the 49 combination-pairs of the seven *sefirot.* Each week of the 49 days corresponds to a *sefirah,* so the first week is *Hesed,* the second week is *Gevurah,* and so on. But each of the seven days in each week is also a *sefirah.* The first day of the first week would be *Hesed* of *Hesed,* the second day would be *Gevurah* of *Hesed,* and so on. In this way, the entire period becomes a rite for invoking the powers of the *sefirot* and channeling them into the world, concluding with revelation at Sinai itself, celebrated with *Shavuot.*

LAG B'OMER

Lag B'Omer is a festival with strong Kabbalah overtones that takes place in the middle of the Counting of the *Omer* period. The Hebrew letters have numeric values, and numbers are written with letters. For example, *lamed,* the "L" sound, is 30; *gimel,* the "G" sound, is three. Thus, *lag* is "33," and *B'Omer* just means "of the *Omer*." So, *Lag B'Omer* is simply the 33rd day of the *Omer* counting.

In terms of the *sefirot,* the 33rd day is *Hod sheba'Hod,* or "Glory of Glory." It could also be rendered "Humility of Humility" or "Gratitude of Gratitude."

Lag B'Omer is a special day in the *Omer* counting for a few reasons. First, it is the *Yom Hillula* (death anniversary) of Rabbi Shimon bar Yokhai. As we learned in chapter 1, Rabbi Shimon is traditionally credited with authorship of the Zohar. According to tradition, before he died, he taught his disciples Kabbalah and instructed them to celebrate his death as "the day of my joy." This is based on the idea that the death of spiritual masters is their wedding day with the Divine. Furthermore, according to tradition, the influence of the spiritual masters in the world actually increases with their death, because their spiritual power is no longer confined to a physical body.

The second reason *Lag B'Omer* is a special day has to do with Rabbi Akiva (whom we also learned about in chapter 1). A story in the Talmud relates how a plague struck the students of Rabbi Akiva at the beginning of the *Omer* period because they lacked respect for one another, and thousands of them died. However, the plague stopped on *Lag B'Omer,* adding the theme of gratitude for Divine compassion on this holy day.

Lag B'Omer is celebrated outdoors with bonfires, music, and festivities. Many devout Jewish pilgrims celebrate in Meron (in Northern Israel), the burial place of Rabbi Shimon bar Yokhai.

SHAVUOT

Shavuot is the festival that concludes the 49-day *Omer* counting period. The Torah simply connects this festival with the process of the growing grain and with farmers offering their first fruits.

The early rabbis, however, taught that *Shavuot* was the day the Children of Israel received the Torah, and particularly the *Aseret HaDibrot,* the "10 Commandments," on Mt. Sinai. According to this rabbinic understanding, *Pesakh* and *Shavuot* came to represent, in Kabbalah, two pillars of the spiritual process: liberation and revelation.

From a Kabbalistic perspective, liberation is not only a historical story of the Israelites going out from Egypt; it is also a story of getting free from the *yetzer hara,* or ego. Ordinarily, we tend to identify ourselves with our thoughts and feelings. Consciousness is "enslaved" in the "Egypt" of ego–that is, the separate self-sense of "me." Liberation, symbolized by the Exodus and celebrated in *Pesakh,* takes us beyond this limited sense of self and into the vast wilderness of the *Ayin,* the field of awareness beyond ego within which the *yetzer tov,* the impulse of Light and Goodness, naturally arises.

While liberation is freedom from thought and feeling, revelation is, from a mystical point of view, a shift in perspective on the nature of thought and feeling. Once we are liberated from the small "me," there is no longer the sense that the thoughts and feelings arising in consciousness are "mine." Rather, they arise from the same place that everything arises from: the Mystery of Being called the Divine. In this way, the arising of thought itself is actually revelation.

This deeper understanding of revelation as a constant process of Divine unfolding is reflected in the way that Jewish law and practice develop over time. While Jewish laws and practices are certainly rooted in the fixed text of the Torah, the understanding and interpretation of that text is not fixed; it is an ever-evolving process. Thus, the dualistic idea of sacred texts like the Bible being "human-made" vs. "God-given" dissolves into the more unitive understanding of One Consciousness, evolving and revealing Itself through us.

Shavuot is traditionally celebrated with the customs of staying up all night and learning the Torah, as well as eating lots of different dairy foods. Milk, as an expression of nurturance, is one of the symbols of Torah. Imagine groups of people gathering to learn sacred texts while eating blintzes!

TISHA B'AV

Finally, *Tisha B'Av* is the anti-holiday; it commemorates the destruction of both the first and second temples, as well as many other horrible tragedies in Jewish History. *Tisha* means "ninth" and *Av* is the name of the month in which it falls, around July. Thus, *Tisha B'Av* simply means the "ninth of *Av*."

Tisha B'Av is observed, like *Yom Kippur,* with a 25-hour complete fast (no food or water). It is a day of extreme mourning. Some practices include not greeting each other and not wearing leather shoes. The main practice is the chanting of *Eikha,* the Book of Lamentations in the Bible, in which the prophet Jeremiah describes the horrors of the first temple's destruction at the hands of the Babylonians. *Tisha B'Av* is the culmination of a longer three-week period of mourning in which observant Jews refrain from music and even eating meat (except for *Shabbat,* on which all mourning is suspended.)

From a mystical point of view, however, *Tisha B'Av* points to the sometimes painful process of destruction and renewal that is part of spiritual growth. Aspirants from all different traditions often go through a period of inner "darkness" prior to one's inner "light" being revealed. This painful experience arises from the fact that sometimes, in order to open up to our deepest Divine nature, we need to experience blocked pain from the past in order to release it. There is a point at which we have to let go of our old selves; the ego has to "die." This ego death is another version of the "plagues in Egypt" story, only in this version, *we* are the Pharaoh experiencing the plagues.

The destruction of the temples, as well as all the other painful experiences of Jewish history, are traditionally linked to our ethical shortcomings; they are the fruits of "bad karma." In

ᧁᦓ   Kabbalah for Beginners

this sense, *Tisha B'Av* points to the understanding that we are responsible for our role in influencing what happens to us, and that our choices have real consequences. But, no matter how far we stray from our Divine nature and no matter how much we suffer, there is an indestructible Divine spark that is ready to be reborn within us. Thus, *Tisha B'Av* leads us back around the yearly cycle to the practice of *teshuvah*, returning to the Divine, and back to the renewal of *Rosh Hashanah* seven weeks later.

FROM FESTIVALS TO PHASES

Now that we've explored the yearly festival cycle and basic practices, let's look at some of the main ways in which Kabbalah has manifested in history. In the next chapter, we'll explore the three major historical phases: Ecstatic Kabbalah, Theosophical Kabbalah, and Hasidism.

CHAPTER FIVE

DIFFERENT SCHOOLS OF KABBALAH

❧

S o far, we have been exploring Kabbalah as a form of mysticism that emerged through the central wellspring of the Zohar. While we mentioned that various schools of Kabbalah interpreted the Zohar differently, the post-Zohar schools still emanated from this common text. This Zohar-based tradition came to be known by modern scholars as Theosophical Kabbalah.

There was another stream of Kabbalah that existed side by side with Theosophical Kabbalah. Scholars call this second stream of Kabbalah the Ecstatic Kabbalah, because its primary focus was on the ecstatic experience of the individual. Of course, the Kabbalah of the Zohar (like all mysticism) was also about ecstatic experience, but the language around that experience was very different in Zohar than in the texts of Ecstatic Kabbalah. As we've seen, the Zohar's language was poetic, speaking in metaphors and allegories in order to describe the inner dynamics of God, rather than the individual. This is why it came to be known as Theosophical Kabbalah; the point of the practice in Zohar is centered around how our actions influence God, rather than how they influence our own *experience* of God.

Out of these two streams emerged, in the 18th century, a totally new type of Jewish mysticism: Hasidism. Unlike the Ecstatic Kabbalah and the Theosophical Kabbalah, which both required a substantial amount of scholarship to practice, Hasidism was a popular movement aimed at the uneducated masses.

In addition to these three movements, it is worth mentioning there also arose a stream of non-Jewish Kabbalah, stemming from the work of certain Christian monks who translated the Zohar and developed their own Christian-based interpretations in the 1500s. This eventually led to the incorporation of Kabbalah into non-Jewish, and also non-Christian, Western mysticism and occultism. We will now explore these different and varied expressions of Kabbalah.

THEOSOPHICAL KABBALAH, ECSTATIC KABBALAH, AND ABULAFIA

The earliest Jewish mystical text that we have, the Sefer Yetzirah, set the stage for both the Theosophical Kabbalah and the Ecstatic Kabbalah. As we saw in chapter 1, the Sefer Yetzirah presents the creation of the universe as happening through "32 Paths of Wisdom." These 32 paths are the 10 *sefirot* and the 22 *otyot*, the Hebrew alphabet.

While the Theosophical Kabbalah focused more on the *sefirot*, the Ecstatic Kabbalah focused more on the *otyot*, the letters. This focus sometimes took the form of uncovering deeper levels of meaning in scriptures through looking at the numerical values of letters and applying other devices such as cyphers. But the main feature of Ecstatic Kabbalah involves a variety of meditation techniques utilizing sound, art, movement, and Hebrew Divine Names to induce shifts in perception and experience. The father of this type of Kabbalah was the legendary 13th-century mystic Abraham Abulafia.

Abulafia was born in Zaragoza, Spain in 1240. (Incidentally, this is the same year that Moses de León of the Zohar was born.) He grew up in Spain and received a traditional rabbinic education, but later immersed himself in philosophy. He became particularly interested in the works of Maimonides, who had combined classical philosophy with Jewish thought about a hundred years earlier.

His life took a radical turn after the death of his father when he was 18. Two years later he set off on a mystical quest to the holy land to find the mythical river, *Sambatyon*. According to a legend in the Talmud, the *Sambatyon* was a wild and rough river on the weekdays, described sometimes as a river of fire and stones, but it would become calm on *Shabbat*.

He didn't find the river, and violence between Muslims and Christians in the holy land caused him to get no further than Akko. From there he fled back to Europe and continued his wanderings in Greece and Italy, eventually returning to Spain for a short time. Some scholars believe that he must have had encounters with Sufi (Muslim) mystics during his wanderings, because his methods, which contained the chanting of Divine names as well as certain yogic breathing exercises, were similar to those practiced by some Sufi sects.

At the age of 31, he had his first transformative mystical experience. He began teaching his methods, which he called "The Way of the Names," to a small group of students.

Abulafia was extremely prolific, writing nearly 50 works in his lifetime on a variety of subjects, including commentaries on both the Sefer Yetzirah and Maimonides' *The Guide for the Perplexed*. His most unique writings, however, were his manuals on achieving mystical prophetic states through highly complex techniques.

The most prominent of these techniques involved the chanting of the "unpronounceable" Divine Name using ever-changing permutations of the letters and vowels. According to Jewish law, it is forbidden to pronounce this Name, but Abulafia apparently ignored this norm. Interestingly, in Jewish Renewal circles today (which we will explore in chapter 6), chanting this traditionally forbidden Name is fairly common in the liturgy.

Besides the fact that this technique went against traditional Jewish law, it was also unique as a meditation method in that it involved a high level of concentration to keep track of the permutations. The method was related to compositional devices in music, in which the composer would use permutations of pitch and rhythm, only this technique permuted sacred letters with vowels and body movements.

Like the heretic Shabbetai Tzvi who came along 400 years later (whom we studied in chapter 1), Abulafia also came to see himself as the Messiah. His messianic claims led to his being exiled from the Jewish community of Messina in Sicily, and he spent the rest of his life on the island of Comino in the Mediterranean, where he wrote his last works.

While Abulafia's messianic claims were not accepted and led to his demise, the techniques he taught had a tremendous influence on Kabbalah over the centuries and continue to influence Kabbalah in all of its many forms today.

HASIDIC KABBALAH

No exploration of Kabbalah would be complete without mentioning what is perhaps the last great flowering of Jewish spirituality in the world, and that is Hasidism.

To understand Hasidism, it's important to know something about the world into which Hasidism was born. Abulafia, Shabbetai Tzvi, and other lesser known Kabbalists with grandiose messianic claims caused great suspicion of Kabbalah in the rabbinic mainstream. The downfall of Shabbetai Tzvi in particular, along with his conversion to Islam, had decimated the spirit of many Jewish communities across Europe.

This served to reinforce the belief that Kabbalah should be hidden from the masses and only taught to accomplished scholars who were prepared for the inner transformations that it induced. While this cautious approach certainly made sense, the downside was that spirituality became inaccessible to the average person. Spirituality was a luxury of the elite. It was into this world that the Hasidic movement was born.

Rabbi Israel ben Eliezer, known as the Baal Shem Tov, began his ministry in 18th-century western Ukraine to remedy this situation. He wrote no books, but his teachings were carried on and written down by his disciples. His teaching, and the lineages that came from him, were known as Hasidism (or *hassidis* in Yiddish) and sought to reveal a core of simplicity in the incredibly complex forms of Kabbalah that had come from Luria and Abulafia.

The essential message was that, since the Divine is ever-present, anyone with a sincere heart can break through the shell of the mundane to the Divine reality that glows softly within all things. You don't have to know a lot of texts, understand the vastly complex structures of Theosophical Kabbalah, or engage in the difficult and dangerous Divine Name permutations of Ecstatic Kabbalah. What you really need, above all else, is a constant awareness of the Divine Presence in this moment. You need to direct your heart, words, and actions to serve the Divine in everything you do. And while this is certainly not easy, *it is simple,* and therefore accessible for both the unlearned and learned alike.

As we learned in chapter 1, this basic practice of Divine awareness and directing oneself to the Divine is called *devekut,* meaning "attaching" or "cleaving" to God. All Jewish mystical practices are aimed at *devekut,* but Hasidism teaches simple, accessible methods for achieving this state which involve the use of emotions, both sorrowful and joyful (with an emphasis on joy), as means to experience and realize the Divine.

Here is a story that illustrates the shift in Hasidism away from the complexities of Kabbalah and toward the simplicity of raw emotion for achieving *devekut:*

Once, the Baal Shem Tov asked his disciple, Ze'ev Wolf Kitzes, to perform the blowing of the *shofar* on *Rosh Hashanah.* The Baal Shem spent many hours teaching him all the Kabbalistic *kavanot* (special mystical formulas) to hold in his mind while blowing the *shofar*, which Wolf wrote down on a slip of paper so that he wouldn't forget.

In the story beginning on page 120, *devekut* was accomplished through the channeling of emotion into the *mitzvah,* the devotional ritual of blowing the *shofar.* It is noteworthy that this particular *mitzvah* involves sound, because another method and probably the most effective of all Hasidic methods involves music: the Hasidic *nigun,* or wordless melody.

A *nigun* is simply a melody that you sing with prayerfulness. Instead of singing words, you sing on any syllable or combination of syllables: *ay dai dai yay yah . . .* whatever works for you.

To begin, bring awareness into your body, your heart, and your gut. Let your awareness rest on the flow of your breathing. Sing a tone. Close your eyes. Let your body sway. Move spontaneously. Build on the tone, either by improvising a melody or by singing one that you know. The idea is to connect with whatever feelings are present, and direct those feelings into the sounds you sing.

Don't worry if you don't sing well or if you don't know much about music. This is not a performance; it is using your voice to prayerfully express whatever feelings are there for you, to draw them out, and, through them, to open yourself more and more to the sacredness of the moment.

Spend some time singing this way, and when you are finished, stay in the silence for some time. When you're ready, open your eyes and behold the wonder of Existence all around and within. You have just sung a *nigun*!

When the time came to blow the *shofar*, Wolf approached the *bima* (where service leaders stood) and reached into his pocket for the slip of paper. But, to his dismay, it was gone! Brokenhearted, he went ahead and blew the *shofar* anyway, with tears running down his cheeks because he had lost the paper and couldn't remember any of the *kavanot*.

Later, the Baal Shem said to him, "Dear heart, you know that there are many keys that open the many rooms in the Divine palace. But there is one tool that is more powerful than any of the keys, and that is the axe! With an axe you can break the locks on any of the doors. That axe is your broken heart . . ."

KABBALAH THEN AND NOW

All of these schools have come to inform the way that Kabbalah has become available today. In the next and final chapter, we will look at how Kabbalah has inspired spiritual movements of the last century and explore how one might draw on this inspiration to create one's own Kabbalah-based spiritual practice.

   Kabbalah for Beginners

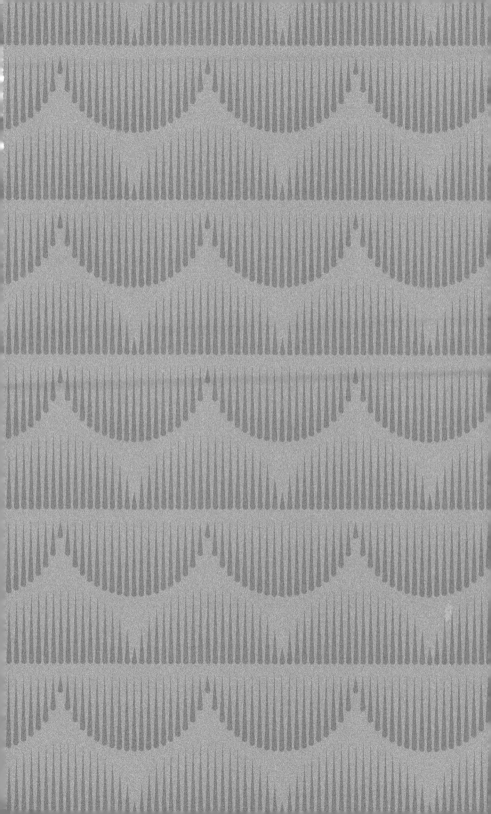

PRESENT-DAY KABBALAH

T he 20th century gave rise to two new trends in Jewish spirituality: one that maintained the symbols and structures of Kabbalah but expressed them in a new and more universal form, and another that left those structures behind to express the *essence* of Jewish spirituality, free from the traditional symbols of Kabbalah.

Neither of these two trends would have been possible without the Hasidic movement that preceded them. This is because Hasidism represented, above all, a popularization of spirituality; it is because of Hasidism that a book on Kabbalah for the general public like this one could be written at all. Hasidism was prophetic; it anticipated the uniquely modern hunger for spirituality that is often experienced as *separate from* and even sometimes as *antithetical to* religion, as in the phrase "spiritual but not religious." This is not to say that Hasidism was anti-religious; Hasidism existed and continues to exist completely within the structures of traditional Judaism. But in its mission to make spirituality available to the masses, it set the stage for the eventual loosening of spirituality from its traditional religious boundaries.

UNIVERSAL KABBALAH AND RENEWAL

In Lodz, Poland, in 1885, Yehuda Ashlag was born into a scholarly Hasidic family. Yehuda was a young prodigy; he studied Kabbalah as well as Talmud as a child, independent of his teachers, and was ordained at the age of 19. As rabbi, he served as a judge in the Jewish courts of Warsaw, but he also learned German and studied secular thinkers such as Marx, Hegel, Schopenhauer, and Nietzsche. It is likely that his exposure to these great non-Jewish thinkers, combined with his in-depth grasp of Lurianic Kabbalah and background in Hasidism, contributed to the eventual development of his radical view of Kabbalah as a universal wisdom that should be available to everyone.

In 1921, Ashlag emigrated with his family to Israel, where he worked as a common laborer by day while secretly writing his Kabbalistic commentaries by night. He was eventually recognized by the chief rabbi of Palestine, Abraham Isaac Kook (himself a Kabbalist), and others for his works on Kabbalah. After this he began to serve again as rabbi, this time in Jerusalem. Among his many works are a translation into Hebrew and commentary on the Zohar called the *Sulam* (Ladder), as well as his book on Lurianic Kabbalah and the 10 *sefirot* called *Talmud Eser Sefirot*.

But perhaps the most well-known influence from Ashlag was his philosophy that Kabbalah should be made available to the world. The Kabbalah Centre, founded in 1965 by Philip Berg and Rabbi Levi Isaac Krakovsky, is the most famous and successful of the many organizations and individual teachers based on Ashlag's work.

Around the same time, another universalist form of Kabbalah was brewing, but in a very different way. Reb Zalman Schachter Shalomi was a *hasid* of the Chabad-Lubavitch movement. He and the famous singing rabbi, Shlomo Carlebach, were among the first rabbis sent out in the 1950s by their *rebbe,* Yosef Yitzchak Schneersohn, to college campuses for the purpose of bringing young Jews back to Judaism.

But by the 1960s, Schachter-Shalomi's encounters with the hippie movement and other spiritual traditions (as well as the consciousness-altering effects of psychedelics) led him to leave Chabad and embrace a more egalitarian and universal world-view. His teaching and leadership gave rise to what came to be known as the Jewish Renewal movement. ("Jewish Renewal" was a term coined by Martin Buber, whom we will learn about in the next section.)

Unlike the Kabbalah Centre, which sought to promote a universal Kabbalah independent of Judaism, Jewish Renewal moved in the other direction. Its aim was (and still is) the renewal and revitalization of spirituality *within* Judaism by applying the teachings of Kabbalah and Hasidism, but also by acknowledging the universal spiritual core within all traditions. In this way,

Jewish Renewal is both tribal and universal at the same time, celebrating the ecumenical and egalitarian movements that were born in the 1960s, while trying to grow and renew the Jewish community through its great spiritual heritage.

I mention Yehuda Ashlag and Reb Zalman Schachter-Shalomi as the forefathers of universal Kabbalah because most other examples of universal Kabbalah today can be traced either directly or indirectly to their influence. The main exception to this is the lineage of non-Jewish Kabbalah mentioned earlier, which comes through the mystery schools and occult traditions of Europe that absorbed elements of Kabbalah as early as the 1500s.

Now let's turn to the other modern trend: those who attempted to express the essential elements of Jewish spirituality free from the complexities of Kabbalistic symbolism.

ESSENTIAL KABBALAH

The universal versions of Kabbalah that descended from Ashlag's philosophy and the universalist Judaism that descended from Reb Zalman represent two different expressions of the universalist trend in Jewish spirituality from the mid- to late 20th century. The essentialist trend also had two different versions—one that sought to throw off not only the symbols and language of Kabbalah, but all the traditional forms of Judaism as well, and one which simply emphasized the essential core *within* the traditional forms of Judaism. These two approaches were embodied in the lives and teachings of two great spiritual geniuses of the 20th century: Martin Buber and Abraham Joshua Heschel.

Martin Buber was born in 1878 into a traditional Jewish family in Vienna. His grandfather, Salomon Buber, was a scholar of rabbinic literature, particularly *midrash*. As a teen, Buber read Kant, Kierkegaard, and Nietzsche, going on to pursue studies in philosophy, philology, and art history. In 1938, he fled Nazi Germany and emigrated to Mandatory Palestine, where he received a professorship at Hebrew University in Jerusalem.

We don't know many details about the inner life of Buber's teen and early adult years, but it seems from his autobiographical writings that he was involved in some mystical practices—maybe Kabbalah, maybe from some other tradition. What is clear is that a kind of crisis occurred which became decisive and foundational for his approach to spirituality and the "formless Judaism" that he promoted.

Buber writes in his autobiographical fragments that people would often come to seek his counsel. One day a young man knocked on his door, disturbing Buber from whatever mystical practice he was involved with. Buber answered the door and spoke to the young man, but he was hasty, as he wanted to get back to whatever he was doing. As a result, Buber "answered the questions he asked but not the questions he didn't ask." A short time after their meeting, Buber learned that the young man had committed suicide.

After this crisis, Buber utterly rejected all formal ritualistic practices. He made it his mission and ultimate goal to always be present with other people, and to make himself available to the deeper reality of what was needed in the moment so that he might never be distracted from serving his fellow human again. In this way, *relationship* became his Judaism.

Buber expanded on this relational approach by publishing many books on Hasidism and Judaism that emphasized this basic principle. His crown work, *Ich und Du* (*I and Thou* or *I and You*), fleshed out his relational, dialogue-based approach in great detail.

For me, Buber is perhaps the most inspiring Jewish thinker of all time because he manages to passionately embody a Judaism that is free from all externally imposed form. In my experience, this would be impossible for most people. In general, people need forms, rituals, and practices to connect with and embody Jewish spirituality. But Buber was different, perhaps way ahead of his time, showing us that freedom from form is possible.

Abraham Joshua Heschel had a similar path to Buber. Born in 1907 in Poland, he, too, was descended from rabbinic families, but with Hasidic dynasties on both sides. Heschel added to his extensive rabbinic training with a study of philosophy at the University of Berlin. And, like Buber, Heschel also fled the Nazis. In 1938, after first being arrested by the Gestapo and deported back to Poland, he made his way to London just six weeks before the German invasion of Poland. His mother and three sisters were all killed by the Nazis.

Heschel arrived in New York City in 1940, and in 1946 he was brought on by the Jewish Theological Seminary as professor of Jewish Mysticism and Ethics. He died in 1972.

Although Heschel's foundations were Hasidism, Kabbalah, and philosophy, his teachings rarely talked in terms of Kabbalistic symbolism. Instead, he focused on the application of Kabbalah in the world and on social transformation.

Both Heschel and Buber are examples of how crisis can give rise to spiritual genius. For Heschel, the crisis of the destruction of his family by the Nazis led him to a profoundly socially and politically engaged Judaism. While Buber's approach was more rooted in the interpersonal, in the "I" to the "You," Heschel's approach was more rooted in the political, inspired by the fiery exhortations of the Hebrew prophets against corruption and oppression. A famous photograph shows Heschel walking with Dr. Martin Luther King Jr. and other civil rights activists in the Selma civil rights march.

Buber and Heschel represent two different expressions of Kabbalah breaking forth from its insular traditional shell into the larger world to effect both individual and societal transformation. They left behind a legacy of inspiring and instructive writings that are must-reads for continuing this transformational work.

EVERYDAY KABBALAH

The central idea of Buber's work *I and Thou* is that we have two modes of existence. The first, called "I-It," is *goal oriented*; we relate to people and things in terms of how they can serve a function. The second, "I-Thou," is *presence oriented*; we relate to beings and things for the sake of the encounter, not for some other agenda. Furthermore, when we relate to beings and things as "thou" rather than "it," we can access the Eternal Thou; that is, the Divine Presence within all beings.

In one of his examples, Buber poetically describes being present with a tree, and in doing so, he actually gives a wonderful instruction for how to practice Presence.

Try it yourself:

Take a walk outside and find a tree to practice with. Walk unhurriedly, noticing your surroundings: the sights, the sounds, the smells. Let the tree call to you; see where you are drawn.

When your tree appears, come into a comfortable position so that you can be present with the tree for some time. You can sit, stand, or lean against the tree.

Then, turn your senses toward the tree. Notice details about the tree, but don't get too drawn into describing the details in your mind. Instead, try and relate to the tree from your heart, giving your attention and simply being in a state of openness and connection with the tree.

Finally, notice that the presence of the tree is the same presence in all things, the same presence that perceives the tree through you. This is the Divine Presence, alive as both you and the tree, knowing Itself through you and the tree.

When you're ready, return to your other activities, enlivened and deepened by this relationship with the Divine Presence.

HOW TO START PRACTICING KABBALAH

Now that we have had a general overview of how Kabbalah has developed and transformed throughout history, let's explore how Kabbalah can become a part of your life and enrich your own spiritual journey. In these final sections, I will share some of what I teach in my own work, as well as offer suggestions for continued study. Everything I share here is suitable for anyone, regardless of background or religious heritage, even though it is based on Judaism. Of course, this only scratches the surface. When you are ready for more, you are welcome to visit my website, TorahOfAwakening.com.

RECOMMENDED READING

Our examination of Kabbalah texts and personalities throughout history has been a very general, high-level survey. The following book recommendations will take you down from this stratospheric view into a closer examination of Kabbalah.

Arthur Green has written a wonderful introductory book called *A Guide to the Zohar* which, in addition to going into more depth on the Zohar, also puts the Zohar in the context of Kabbalah and history in general. It is not difficult to read, even though it is dense and probably has more information than the average person might easily digest.

Arthur Green was also the editor of an amazing series called *Jewish Spirituality*, in two volumes. The first takes you from Biblical times through the Middle Ages, and the second takes you from the 16th century to the present (the "present" being 1987). The great thing about this survey is that each chapter is written by a different author, so not only do you get an in-depth overview of Jewish spirituality, you also get to sample many great authors who are well-versed in the subject.

Green's guide was released in conjunction with a new translation of the Zohar itself by Professor Daniel Matt. Matt's Zohar is replete with commentary and notes that explain the Zohar's particular symbolism and literary references. Matt also wrote a little book called *The Essential Kabbalah: The Heart of Jewish Mysticism*, which is a short collection of Kabbalistic texts translated into English, and is another wonderful way to sample the spectrum of Kabbalistic writings.

Green and Matt both write with sensitivity and love for the spirituality of Kabbalah, without any particular religious agenda. The tone of the books is scholarly. Rabbi Aryeh Kaplan, on the other hand, writes from a traditional, Orthodox point of view. Nevertheless, his work as a translator and emissary of Kabbalah to the English-speaking world has been unparalleled. I highly recommend his book *Meditation and Kabbalah*, which translates and explains many different Kabbalistic text excerpts, with the aim of demonstrating several meditation methods.

Kaplan also translated two key texts, both of which are fairly short (as opposed to the Zohar). The Sefer Yetzirah and the Bahir are core texts that we can now read in English, thanks to Rabbi Aryeh Kaplan.

Like Kaplan, Reb Zalman Schachter-Shalomi also wrote as a scholar, religious leader, and spiritual teacher, but not from an Orthodox point of view. Rather, Zalman's writings bring you into the contemporary world of Renewal and Neo-Hasidism. His first book, *Gate to the Heart: A Manual of Contemplative Jewish Practice*, is considered to be the first English manual of Jewish meditation ever written. Other books worth checking out for the beginner are *Paradigm Shift* and *A Heart Afire: Stories and Teachings of the Early Hasidic Masters*.

Finally, my own book, *Integral Jewish Meditation - Three Portals of Presence for Spiritual Awakening*, teaches the simple but in-depth transformative meditation that we practice in the Torah of Awakening online community, while laying down the foundational teachings of Kabbalah in a way that is practical and applicable.

Of course, there are thousands more books to explore, but in my experience, these are a great place to begin. Now let's move on from reading materials to the practices themselves.

GUIDED MEDITATION

Here's a meditation based on the three *sefirot* of *Hesed* (loving-kindness), *Gevurah* (strength), and *Tiferet* (beauty, grace, radiance).

In this meditation, we'll be chanting the Hebrew words, *l'kha, na'aseh v'nishma. L'kha* comes from the Biblical verse that says,

> L'kha Hashem Hagedulah—For you, O God, is the Greatness . . .

> (CHRONICLES 29:11)

The rest of this verse is the source for the names of the different *sefirot,* including *Gevurah, Tiferet, Netzakh,* and *Hod. Hagedulah* is understood in Kabbalah to refer to *Hesed,* loving-kindness. *L'kha* means "for you" or "to you," and so is an offering word, embodying the spirit of *Hesed.*

Na'aseh v'nishma comes from the story of the Israelites receiving Divine revelation at Mt. Sinai:

> And the people said, everything that the Divine speaks, na'aseh v'nishma, we will do and we will hear.

> EXODUS, 24:7

Come into a comfortable position. You can be seated, standing, or lying down on your back.

We'll begin by awakening the energy of the *Hesed* in the heart. First, take a nice deep breath. Now place your right hand on your heart and bring your awareness there, imagining a light shining from your heart center. Offer your attention and presence lovingly to this moment, to Existence *as* this moment, and chant the offering word *l'kha* on a long outbreath.

Next, invoke *Gevurah* by bringing your left hand down to your belly, seeing your organs radiant with light. Feel downward from there into your hips, down into your thighs, knees, calves, feet, and toes.

Shine your awareness upward into your chest, outward into your shoulders, down your arms, and into your hands. Then, let your awareness rise upward into your head, shining into your face, bringing your lips to a little smile to express generosity of Presence, filling your whole body with the light of awareness. Rest your attention in the flow of your breathing. Anchor your body awareness by chanting the word *na'aseh* on a long outbreath.

Now, with open heart and embodied awareness, we transcend beyond the physical and the emotional to *Tiferet,* the open field of awareness itself.

To do this, bring your right hand up from your heart and touch your fingers to your forehead. Expand your awareness from your body outward into the space around you, noticing whatever objects and beings are present, as well as the sounds and the lighting.

Next, notice the awareness itself–that which is aware of your body, your feelings, your senses, and everything around you, including sounds, sensations, and open space. Notice that *you are this awareness,* beyond your body, beyond your thoughts, beyond your feelings, beyond your sensations. This is *Tiferet,* the radiant beauty of awareness itself within which everything in this moment arises. Affirm your identity with awareness by chanting *v'nishma* on a long outbreath.

Let yourself fall into the boundless depths of this moment, simply being present.

When you're ready, kiss your fingertips, then relax your arms and take a nice breath. Return to your ordinary activities, refreshed and awakened.

DAILY STUDY

As we learned in chapter 4, a wonderful and succinct formula for living a spiritual life was expressed by the sage Shimon the Righteous in the Mishnaic text, Pirkei Avot. There he says that the world stands on three things: *Torah, Avodah,* and *Gemilut Hasadim:* learning, spiritual practice, and acts of loving-kindness.

First, let's look briefly at *Gemilut Hasadim,* "acts of loving-kindness." While kindness is basically self-explanatory, there are two ways in which kindness is traditionally expressed that are worth noting: the giving of charity (*tzedakah*) and refraining from harmful speech (*lashon hara*).

I mention these two because they are such powerful practices, yet so easy to ignore. Speaking gossip and slander about others is particularly commonplace and takes extra effort to eliminate from your life habits, but eliminating it is highly beneficial both to yourself and others. The *mitzvah* of giving *tzedakah,* charity, is considered a basic, non-optional responsibility. The practice is to tithe oneself, traditionally 10 percent of your income, and give it to those in need. While these two practices are of course not the whole of *Gemilut Hasadim,* they are a great place to start.

The most important thing about daily study is that you make it part of your daily routine. It says in the Mishna (Peah 1:1), *"These are the things that have no prescribed measure . . . acts of kindness and Torah study."* In other words, there is no set amount of kindness one must do or material that one must study. If you have 20 minutes, you could study one book in depth for 20 minutes, or you could study six books; it depends on how you learn and what works best for you. Personally, I am constantly adjusting the number of texts I study every day, as the conditions of my life change. The crucial thing is to do it every day.

In selecting what texts to learn, one method is to select from different historical periods. I would break these down very broadly into five categories: Biblical, rabbinic, classical Kabbalah, Hasidic, and contemporary.

A great way to study Biblical text is according to the traditional weekly readings. In Judaism, a portion of the Torah is read in synagogue every week. Each portion is called a *parshah,* and each has a name that comes from the opening of the *parshah.*

It's important to understand that one of the most important contributions of Kabbalah is its radical reinterpretation of scripture in which the narratives and laws are seen as "coverings" concealing, but also poetically revealing, mystical secrets. As you become familiar with the Biblical narratives, keep in mind that the point is not necessarily to take them literally, but to internalize the textual ocean in which Kabbalah swims. Once you get some familiarity with the texts, you might even try applying your own creativity, contemplating the passages and seeing what insights emerge. A good way to do this is to alternate between reading passages and sitting quietly, taking a receptive attitude and asking questions of yourself to see what comes.

For rabbinic text, my favorite for study is Pirkei Avot, which I have quoted numerous times in this book. Pirkei Avot is a short wisdom text contained in the Mishna, and many Jewish prayer books (*siddurim*) contain it. Pirkei Avot consists of short aphorism-like pieces, each called a *mishna*, and a good way to study it is to contemplate one *mishna* per day.

As for classical Kabbalah, I mentioned Daniel Matt's translation of the Zohar, which comes in 10 volumes and will keep you learning for years to come. Aryeh Kaplan's Sefer Yetzirah and Bahir translations are also wonderful.

For Hasidic literature, the most widely translated text is the Tanya, written by Rabbi Shneur Zalman of Liadi in the late 1700s. Some of the material in the Tanya may seem strange and alienating to the modern mind, but there is a lot in this text that is wonderful. A good contemporary and non-Orthodox introduction to the Tanya is *Tanya, the Masterpiece of Hasidic Wisdom* by Rabbi Rami Shapiro. Martin Buber's *Tales of the Hasidim* Volumes I and II are classic for Hasidic stories.

As for contemporary writers, any of the authors I mentioned in the "Recommended Reading" section on page 132 are great places to start. In addition, Abraham Joshua Heschel, whom I mentioned under Essential Kabbalah (see page 128), wrote a classic must-read called *The Sabbath*.

Once you make daily study part of your life, you will come to appreciate the gift of spiritual and intellectual growth that comes from this vitally important habit. The principle of daily study can really be applied to anyone studying any subject, but it is especially core for anyone wanting to grow in Kabbalah.

DAILY BLESSINGS AND PRAYERS

One of the most basic techniques for bringing the inner light that you access during meditation into all of your daily activities is through the use of *brakhot*, or blessings. In Judaism, there are blessings for all kinds of activities, from sleeping to waking, eating to using the bathroom, for getting dressed, for learning Torah, for seeing something special in nature, and many more.

For the beginner, a great place to start is the prayer that is traditionally chanted the moment you wake up in the morning:

Modeh (*Modah* in the feminine) *ani l'fanekha, melekh hai v'kayam, shehekhezarta bi nishmati b'khemla, raba emunatekha!*

Here's a rough translation: "I give thanks to You, Eternal, All-Pervading Life. You return my awareness to me with compassion; abundant is Your faithfulness."

Let's look at each of the Hebrew words to get a sense of their inner meaning. The first word is *modeh* in the masculine form, *modah* in the feminine. (Like many languages, Hebrew is gendered, so a male would say *modeh* and a female would say *modah.*) *Modeh* or *modah* means "thanks." Saying *modeh* or *modah* the moment you wake up begins the day with the recognition that your very existence is a gift.

The word *modeh* or *modah* also means "surrender." For example, if two people were in an argument and one conceded that the other was right, the one who surrendered would be *modeh* or *modah* to the other. So, as we awaken to the new day, we are reminded to check within and consciously release any resistance we might feel, surrendering to the truth of the moment.

The next two words are *ani,* which means "I," and *l'fanekha,* which means "before You." Together, the opening three words mean, "I give thanks before You."

The next word is *melekh,* "king." Nowadays, the "king" metaphor may seem antiquated and patriarchal. Some English *siddurim* (prayer books) translate this as "sovereign." Above, I have translated it as "All-Pervading" in order to avoid the connotations of "king."

However, *melekh* actually means more than just "king"; it means specifically one who is empowered to be king by the subjects they rule. A king who takes control by force would be called a *moshal,* not a *melekh.* So, in saying "king" we are consciously making the Divine "king" of our lives; we are "putting God on the throne" in a sense, and taking our egos off the throne.

The next word is *Hai,* which means "living." (The underlined H is pronounced with a guttural sound, like "Bach," and the vowel is like "eye"). Then comes *v'kayam,* which means "and enduring," or literally "standing." These two words describe the "king" as "living and enduring." The idea here is that reality is not something dead, nor is it temporary. Things and beings live and die, come in and out of existence, but Existence Itself cannot be destroyed. It is not a thing that comes and goes.

The next phrase, *"shehekhezarta bi nishmati, b'khemla,"* means "You have returned to me my soul (awareness) with compassion." With this we recognize the miraculous gift of our life as it is renewed in this moment. Then, *raba emunatekha,* "abundant is your faithfulness." Rather than take for granted that we awaken each morning, we view this daily occurrence as a gift.

Try chanting these words while you are still lying in bed in the morning. When you do, notice your inner state. Be aware of any residual thoughts and feelings from your dreams. Bring attention to your breathing, feeling the aliveness within your body and the flow of your breath in and out. Then chant the words with a melody or on a single pitch, or simply whisper them softly.

If you are new to Hebrew, it will take some time to become comfortable pronouncing the words. But if you stick with it, not only will you become comfortable with the words, you will develop a positive habit that will add depth and warmth to your whole day. When that happens, you may want to take on another daily blessing. Traditionally there are 100 blessings to be said every day, and you can learn them all, one step at a time. For a complete course on the daily prayers, as well as instruction in Kabbalah meditation both for beginners and for advanced practitioners, you're invited to visit me at TorahOfAwakening.com.

I hope this book has whet your appetite for discovering the Light within the depths of your own being and for accessing this Light through the teachings and practices of Kabbalah. There is so much more, and I bless you that this should be an entry point for continuing growth and awakening to your full spiritual potential!

INDEX

ACKNOWLEDGMENTS

All gratitude to those without whom this work would not be possible:

Thanks to Reb Zalman Schachter-Shalomi *z"l* (may his memory be for blessing) for supporting my learning and development throughout my life. Thanks to Dr. Rabbi Avram Davis for training me in the world of Jewish meditation, giving me the opportunity to teach, and being a tremendous support through difficult times. Thanks to Shaykh Ibrahim Baba (may his secret be sanctified) for spiritual guidance and friendship. Special thanks to Rabbis Burt Jacobson, Diane Elliot, SaraLeya Schley, David Zaslow, Chai Levy, Riqi Kosovske, David Seidenberg, and Avi Alpert for ongoing support of Torah of Awakening. Most of all, thanks to my wife Lisa, my parents Peg Muller and Dr. Michael Schachter, and my parents-in-love Norman and Bonnie Brooks for ever-flowing love, support, and guidance.

ABOUT THE AUTHOR

BRIAN YOSEF SCHACHTER-BROOKS is a Jewish spiritual teacher and musician. He has been teaching on Kabbalah and the practice of Presence (meditation, mindfulness) since 2006. He received *s'miha* (ordination) as *Minister of Sacred Music* (*Reb Yosef Briah Zohar, Menatzeiakh, Ba'al Tefilah*) from Reb Zalman *z"l* (2012), *Spiritual Teacher and Awakener of Souls* (*Morei Rukhani uM'oreir N'shamot*) from Shaykh Ibrahim Baba Farajaje (may his secret be sanctified) and Rabbi SaraLeya Schley (2012), and certification to teach Jewish meditation (*Moreh L'hitbodedut*) from Dr. Avram Davis (2004). He is the author of *Integral Jewish Meditation - Three Portals of Presence for Spiritual Awakening*, and founded the online Kabbalah meditation community, Torah of Awakening, in 2016. Learn more at TorahOfAwakening.com.

Printed in the USA
CPSIA information can be obtained
at www.ICGtesting.com
CBHW041729160424
6994CB00012B/210